PERFECT FOOL
THE LIFE AND CAREER OF
Ed Wynn

BY GARRY BERMAN

PERFECT FOOL: THE LIFE AND CAREER OF ED WYNN
©2012 GARRY BERMAN

ALL RIGHTS RESERVED.

No part of this book may be reproduced in any form or by any means, electronic, mechanical, digital, photocopying, or recording, except for in the inclusion of a review, without permission in writing from the publisher.

Published in the USA by:

BEARMANOR MEDIA
P.O. BOX 71426
ALBANY, GEORGIA 31708
www.BearManorMedia.com

ISBN-10: 1-59393-676-1 (alk. paper)
ISBN-13: 973-1-59393-676-1 (alk. paper)

Printed in the United States of America.

BOOK DESIGN AND LAYOUT BY VALERIE THOMPSON

TABLE OF CONTENTS

ACKNOWLEDGMENTS **1**

INTRODUCTION **3**

CHAPTER 1: Born Funny **9**

CHAPTER 2: The Rising Star **19**

CHAPTER 3: Hitting the Big Time **29**

CHAPTER 4: The Mother of Invention **43**

CHAPTER 5: The Toast of Broadway **59**

CHAPTER 6: The Fire Chief **69**

CHAPTER 7: Disappointments **87**

CHAPTER 8: The Stage, the Wives, and the Troops **95**

Chapter 9:	Waiting in the Wings **115**
Chapter 10:	TV Or Not TV **125**
Chapter 11:	Out With The Old **147**
Chapter 12:	A Star Is Reborn **159**
Chapter 13:	Better With Age **173**

Epilogue **185**

Notes **187**

Bibliography **205**

Index **209**

ACKNOWLEDGMENTS

Thanks to those who provided helpful contributions to my research: Aaron Neathery, Millie Perkins, Tracy Wynn, Craig Zavetz, Jim Davidson, the staff of the Philadelphia Free Public Library, and the staff of New York Public Library for the Performing Arts at Lincoln Center. A special thank-you to Ben Ohmart, Sandy Grabman, and the ever-patient and talented Valerie Thompson.

All photos are from the author's personal collection, unless otherwise noted.

INTRODUCTION:
A FORGOTTEN CLOWN

They called him "The Master." For the entire first half of the twentieth century, he delighted audiences in theatres, on radio, and on television with his combination of corny verbal comedy and clever sight gags, delivered with a personal charm that few clowns since have possessed.

But while countless comedians through the years have reached the highest tiers of show business with their abilities to make audiences laugh, only a precious few are still hailed as today true icons of American comedy: Chaplin, Keaton, Laurel and Hardy, the Marx Brothers, and W.C. Fields top the list without question. They've all been gone for decades, but we still know them and enjoy their brilliance. Their faces and comedic legacy have become enmeshed in our popular culture. It is ironic then, that the man these comedy greats had themselves referred to as the Master is rarely listed among them. Ed Wynn was his name, and by reviewing his long career, it is easy see how he was perhaps the quintessential American comedian—and arguably the most popular of his time.

At first glance, it might appear that Ed was just another vaudeville-style clown, with a rubbery face and giggly voice, who dispensed corny jokes while wearing silly costumes (including a collection of hats that numbered over eight hundred). There was much more to him than that. He took his comedy seriously, and was a lifelong student of the art. Evidence of this can be found in an argument he once made while addressing a long-held theory that there were only seven basic jokes, from which all others throughout comedy history are descended. "I have done a lot of research on this legend," Ed said. "I have collected a library of 17,000 volumes of jokes, humorous stories and folk tales of all nations, and for a hobby I put in eleven years boiling down 9000 of these jokes until I got a hundred basic ones—and not one had the faintest family relation to another."

It was Ed who coined this famous definition of a comedian: "A comedian is not a man who says funny things; a comedian is a man who says things funny." He did both, and he did it for longer than most of his peers in comedy. In fact, it could be argued that he had five careers in one: as a vaudeville and Ziegfeld *Follies* comedian, the Perfect Fool on stage (so named from one of his self-produced revues), radio's *Fire Chief* (the popular Texaco-sponsored radio program), an early pioneer on television, and finally, in his later years, a highly acclaimed dramatic character actor. With each major development in American entertainment, and with each new invention further expanding communication for the masses, Ed was at the head of the line, always expanding his impressive list of credentials. Off-stage, he was a dignified, somewhat somber man whose private life allowed for precious few laughs. He occasionally acknowledged his personal tribulations, but never asked for pity.

Even with his numerous professional accomplishments and popularity with the public, it is often said that a true measure of success in any field of endeavor is achieving the respect and admiration of one's peers. In Ed's case, while winning the raves of audiences and critics alike (one of his biggest fans was longtime *New York Times* theatre critic J. Brooks Atkinson), he attained a level of praise from his contemporaries in show business rarely matched by any other comedian since. A few examples:

JACK BENNY: "I have always thought that Ed Wynn was the world's greatest comedian, and I still think there is nobody that has ever been as funny or will be, in my time, as he was in his heyday."

EDDIE CANTOR: "'The Perfect Fool' for more than a half-century. His lisp, his hands, his familiar chuckle, his good clean fun for the whole family, his adherence to the rule that jokes obscene should not be heard, stamps him as the stage comedian of the century."

GROUCHO MARX: "Friday night [I saw] the Ed Wynn show. Utterly delightful, a master comic, not a dirty line or joke in the entire two and a half hours."

JERRY LEWIS: "To steady his hand, [a comic has] got to be a serious man…to get up there and make a fool of himself. Ed Wynn, of course, is the prime example."

DONALD O'CONNOR: "Ed Wynn was one of the greatest comedians and actors that ever lived."

In 2007, legendary TV comedy producer Norman Lear wrote, "Any century is lucky if it has a clown or two, the last century had Ed Wynn. Not a comic, a clown. *The Ed Wynn Show*, starring this genius, this clown, [was] a must see in the earliest days of black and white television…"

This begs the question: If Ed Wynn was such a major figure in the world of comedy for so long, why is he rarely remembered today?

To begin with, there's the question of timing. The majority of his successes took place on the stage and before World War II; first in vaudeville (in the *Ziegfeld Follies*), and then as the creative force behind his many Broadway revues. Unfortunately, none of these stage productions were adapted for film or recorded for posterity (the one exception, *Manhattan Mary*, was not Ed's own creation). As his radio career flourished, however, his verbal comedy *was* recorded, thankfully, and has since been released on albums, CDs, and has found its way onto a number of on-line radio archives.

Another factor that has worked against Ed's lasting prominence in the annals of comedy history is his career on television. Television has, for the past sixty years, been the unofficial guardian of our pop culture's collective memory. It is the medium through which that memory is most commonly shared and passed down from one generation to the next. The sad truth is that if an entertainer's best work from many decades ago isn't easily available to see on TV Land, on DVD, or on YouTube, it stands a good chance of being forgotten altogether. Without television to record, preserve, and present a comedian's work to new generations, that performer is almost assured a slow drift into obscurity. Stop almost anyone on the street today and ask about Jackie Gleason or Lucille Ball and you're likely to hear the instant connection made to *The Honeymooners* and *I Love Lucy*. Reruns have enabled those stars to solidify their niche in our collective consciousness simply by never having left it.

Ed's variety show, produced at the dawn of network television, has been preserved on video, and can be purchased on several on-line web sites. However, his program exists only on crude, grainy kinescopes. In the days before videotape, kinescopes were made by essentially pointing a film camera at a studio monitor, and filming it during a live TV broadcast. But our favorite comedy programs from the 1950s that are still rerun today are not kinescoped variety shows, but cleaner looking filmed sitcoms. Ed's show remains valuable because it so closely resembled his many legendary stage successes from the 1920s and 1930s. But although his show has been preserved, only individuals who seek it out are likely to find it.

Ironically, it is easier to see Ed today in several of his more *dramatic* roles in productions such as *The Diary of Anne Frank*, the television version of *Requiem for a Heavyweight*, and the two episodes of *The Twilight Zone* (all of which are available on DVD). And then there is, of course, his memorable if brief appearance as Uncle Albert in Disney's *Mary Poppins*, and as the voice of the Mad Hatter in the animated *Alice In Wonderland*.

Another possible reason why recent comedy historians have overlooked Ed is that his brand of comedy had simply worn out its welcome by the mid-1950s. Comedy at that time began to head in a new direction, led by social satirists and stand-up comedians in suits. Ed refused to change the clownish persona he had created decades earlier, and consequently he failed to meet with changing times and tastes. This was no crime, of course. Steve Martin once reflected on the lasting value of any given comedy style, even after it has been deemed obsolete. "Unlike as in most of the arts," Martin wrote, "greatness in comedy is not necessarily judged by its ability to transcend generations. Comedy is designed to make people laugh now, not three generations later...But just because it isn't funny now doesn't mean it wasn't funny then."

Silent comedy legend Harold Lloyd offered a similar take on the sentiment: "It is sure that some jokes that made our grandparents laugh do not seem especially funny to us," he wrote. "But on the other hand, many of the same joke situations that convulse us today—on the screen, radio or television—also made our grandparents, and their grandparents before them, rock and roll with laughter."

It can even be argued that some comedians who *did* try to tinker with their image in an effort to update it met with poor results. Ed stayed true to what he knew best, but in the end suffered for it, giving him little choice but to retire—that is, until his new career as a character actor took off.

His style of comedy could be found in the acts of later-generation clowns, whether they realized it or not, such as Soupy Sales, Pee Wee Herman, Gallagher, and Carrot Top (the latter two featuring offbeat prop "inventions" in their acts, just as Ed had throughout his career). Of course, the breadth and depth of Ed's talents far exceeded those of these like-minded successors.

Comedy and the desire to make audiences laugh was Ed's obsession, and for that alone he deserves to be remembered for his remarkable career. He was among those past masters who lived, breathed, and dreamed comedy, always striving to create new means of filling theatres with laughter.

At this, Ed Wynn indeed succeeded as few others have.

Chapter 1: Born Funny

"No one has yet to determine, to my satisfaction, what elements of nature, genetics, and environment have to combine to form a man or woman with a keen sense of humor."
—Neil Simon

Imagine transporting yourself back in time to the early years of the twentieth century. It is November of 1908. You arrive unnoticed in the back of the Colonial Theatre in New York City. On the stage stands a young comedian in his early twenties, wearing a big, floppy Panama hat. But he isn't only wearing it—as he regales the crowd with well-timed patter, he demonstrates how the hat can be folded into a seemingly limitless variety of shapes. The spectacle has the audience responding with waves of laughter. There's something about his youthful confidence and good-natured silliness that appeals to the patrons and theatre critics alike. The young man's name appears on the bill as Ed Wynn.

At that time, there were no movie theatres to attend for most people (the first such theatre having opened only three years earlier). There were no radio programs to listen to. Sound recordings were etched onto hard wax cylinders, as record disks were still years away. The concept of television was still new even to science fiction and fantasy writers. However, professional entertainers did have an established home, and it was on the stage. Vaudeville stage shows treated audiences not only with comedians, but parades of singers, dancers, jugglers, animal tamers, whatever the imagination could conjure. And any combination of such performers could be seen on a single bill on any given night. A vaudeville show was a colorful splash of entertainment and energy that kept rolling from one act to another, be it a hit or a flop, with a momentum that didn't cease until the final curtain fell.

As evidenced by his observation quoted at the top of this chapter, Neil Simon may not be certain to what degree a comedian is born or made. If it's the former, then the world became a lot funnier as of November 9, 1886, with the birth of Isaiah Edwin Leopold in Philadelphia, to parents Joseph and Minnie.

Joseph Leopold was a Bohemian Jew who, upon his arrival in America among the throngs of his fellow Eastern Europeans, set out to make a new life for himself. He met and married his wife Minnie, who was born near Istanbul and moved to America with her parents when she was still a child. Joseph and Minnie put down roots in Philadelphia and established a millinery, making and selling women's hats at their store, at 2516 Kensington Avenue. They led a solid, middle-class life for that time, living comfortably above the store. Indeed, Joseph had discarded nearly all traditional European Jewish observances and traditions as he began his life anew.

The Leopold's built a thriving family business, J. Leopold & Co., which included a shop at 702 Arch Street run by a cousin and one-time Philadelphia councilman, Morris Apt. Joseph and Minnie also brought their oldest son, Leon, into the business at a young age.

With the arrival of younger son Isaiah Edwin—nicknamed "Izzy" by the family—Joseph saw yet another heir to the family millinery empire. But his plan would run into an unexpected obstacle even before Izzy reached his teens.

As a child, Izzy always wanted to be funny. And he was. Thinking of ways to make people laugh occupied his mind throughout most of his waking hours. Unlike many comedians, his desire to perform wasn't the result of a sudden epiphany by watching a successful comedian entertain a delighted crowd. Nor was it a casual interest that slowly grew over time. Izzy's keen sense of humor was just *there*, virtually from the beginning, and he was cognizant of it, and indulged himself without the need of prodding from others. "As a young boy," he said, "I had a great sense of the ridiculous, and I understood jokes way beyond the average young man's comprehension. I mean a joke. I'm not speaking now of witty sayings. I'm speaking of real jokes that I could write, and did write." He would often borrow a ladies hat from his father's shop inventory and give impromptu performances for customers, family, and friends, just for the sake of getting laughs. He thrived on the attention and approval of his audiences.

As he entered his teen years, Iz especially enjoyed the summer vacations the family spent in Atlantic City. There he unabashedly sought the attention of beach goers with his shtick, often leading a group of other attention-seeking boys in performances they had seen on the famed Steel Pier stages. One of their recreations was a lion-taming act, "Angie and her Lions," with Izzy as the lead and his beach friends as the snarling lions. These hastily-prepared sketches helped him nurture his innate sense of the ridiculous. His was a genuine comic sense, a creative sense, one in which he took pride even at that young age. "I used to be the biggest attraction on that beach in the morning," he recalled. "I will never forget it. At Virginia Avenue where the Steel Pier is, they would hang on the boardwalk and go to the pier and watch us. That I know for a fact because those were my first press notices."

Izzy began his real theatrical career at the age of 14, in Textile Hall in Philadelphia. He worked for a brief time for no pay, and played different musical instruments while going through a comedy patter routine (according to one story, he went on the road briefly—and without parental permission—as assistant to a medicine man called Chief White King). Regardless of the modest or offbeat performing opportunities available to him at the time, his unshakable desire to entertain the public conflicted greatly with his father's hopes and plans for him. Firstly, Joseph wanted Iz to get an education, at least through high school, while at the same time participating in the family business. This was always expected of him—a point Joseph was sure to reiterate whenever Izzy's attention began to wander elsewhere, especially toward his fondness of silly, clownish behavior. But Joseph's efforts were to prove futile. His son was interested only in making people laugh.

It isn't surprising that Izzy's sense of humor was lost on his parents' Old World sensibilities. "My whole family was manufacturers of ladies hats…I never got any theatrical ability or encouragement from anyone in my family," he said. "I have had people say I was the funniest guy in school you ever saw. No, I did not get it from a nice little cultivated Jewish family, as I think my father and mother were."

When the Ballabazoo Club, a local amateur theatrical society consisting of Y.M.H.A. members, accepted Izzy for membership at fifteen, his enthusiasm for clowning took a sharp upward turn. He now had a place to go where he could be with like-minded people who could teach him the ropes, even if they themselves weren't necessarily destined for the big time. "I was not a singer," he said. "I was not a dancer. So I became a student of comedy…how to make an audience laugh."

The deeper Izzy delved into show business, the harder Joseph fought to have his son pursue more serious endeavors. But it wasn't long before Izzy began presenting himself as a professional entertainer, even as Joseph enrolled him in the University of Pennsylvania to take the Wharton Business Course. Predictably enough, rather than concentrating on his studies, the reluctant student found a far greater satisfaction performing in the university's Mask and Wig talent show. He was a hit with everyone, except his father.

In his book *Ed Wynn's Son*, Keenan Wynn describes the first germ of publicity his father managed to get into print. "There is a crumbling newspaper clipping," Keenan reports, "One of Dad's first. It tells of a young Leopold, 'college graduate, clubman, and author' announcing that 'he had decided to give up all claim on his father's wealth and would devote the rest of his life to theatricals as playwright and actor.'" For a mere teenager, it was a brash introduction indeed.

Joseph Leopold, with his insistence that Izzy join the family business, found himself outnumbered by those who provided a structured outlet for his son's creativity. Still, Joseph continued to lecture on the importance of an education over show business.

The tug of war continued. In 1902, Izzy caught wind of a traveling outfit, the Thurber-Nasher 10-20-30 Repertory Company, which was about to begin a road tour in Connecticut (the 10-20-30 referred to the ticket prices. Thirty cents bought the best seats in the house). Not yet sixteen at the time, but firmly convinced that life on the stage was the life for him, he left home to join the company, ingratiating himself with the troupe without so much as a formal invitation. They played week-long stands with a nightly change of bill, performing eleven shows a week. Izzy received $12 a week for doing whatever he was told to do, such as giving out handbills on the street. But he wouldn't be truly happy until he could convince theatre managers to put him onstage.

It was commonplace for aspiring young vaudeville comedians like Izzy to have lacked the life experience or comic know-how necessary to present an original, polished act right off the bat. Many would try to break into the business merely by presenting out-and-out imitations of more established performers. Anything to keep the audience laughing and the theatre manager satisfied. Vaudeville was teeming with comedy acts of all kinds. The law of the jungle ruled, although, unlike the jungle, not only the fittest survived; the not-so-fit were somehow able to travel the circuits for some time as well, before finally opting for a saner lifestyle. The best thing about it was that a comedian performing for a different audience two or three times each day could experiment with the act, and test new ideas. If he bombed in Chicago, he could make changes and be a hit a few days later in Kansas City. There was no shortage of audiences willing to give each act a chance before rendering their verdict.

The only act Izzy had worked out was an imitation of ethnic comedian Joe Welch, who donned the garb and accent of a Hasidic Jew for his schtick. Having learned all of Welch's monologue, the novice performer was eager for a tryout before an audience. The management gave him a slot at Haverhill, Massachusetts on August 8, 1902.

Lew Fields, a legendary vaudeville comedian (along with his longtime partner Joe Weber) once said, "Make-up is good for an entrance. It gets a laugh when you come on, and that's a good beginning. After that, you must work." This was something young Izzy was about to learn the hard way.

"The only original thing in the monologue was my 'entrance,' so to say," he later wrote. "I was seated on a box in front of the 'drop in one,' holding a newspaper before my face, when the curtain went up and the orchestra played *Wearing of the Green*. Then I let the paper down and there I was in the regulation make-up of the orthodox Jewish comedian. It was a laugh. Then I began. Well, I was just hissed and booed off the stage. I must have been dreadful to affect an audience so. I never finished the monologue."

Despite the dispiriting performance, he stayed with the troupe until the company ran out of money. "After nineteen weeks the thing folded," he said, "stranded in Bangor, Maine. Nobody could get out of town and the state of Maine was always a dry state. I played the piano—only sixteen years of age—in a whorehouse, practically, to get the money to leave."

He made his way back home humbled from this first foray into life as a traveling entertainer. His options, as always, were either to join the family business, or try again to create some sort of foothold for himself in show business.

By 1903, there were two thousand vaudeville theatres in North America, and the number was still growing. Benjamin Franklin Keith and partner Edward Albee's first vaudeville show to be labeled as such opened in Boston in 1882. In 1894, the team opened their ornate Colonial Theatre in Boston. The theatre set a standard for opulence among the bigger vaudeville houses throughout the country, where ordinary customers, in such lavish surroundings, could feel as privileged as wealthy patrons, but were charged a modest admission fee. In addition, Keith devised the two-a-day format for the big-time houses, in which a full bill of entertainment acts was presented twice a day. A more continuous three-a-day format was established for the small-time theatres.

Vaudeville shows evolved into highly structured presentations. Generally, the first act on a bill would usually be a visual, action-oriented act, such as acrobats and jugglers who would not have to rely on dialogue as noisy latecomers entered the theatre. A song-and-dance team or comedy team would follow, then a musical number, and so on. Star performers would close the first act before intermission, and a grand finale would close the show, leaving a favorable lasting impression for the departing audience. Each performer would appear only once per show, and the acts were given equal time—about ten to twenty minutes—to do their thing.

Unfortunately, the only record we have of vaudeville's great comedy performances are in the form of rarely seen silent and sound films, some of which were made for the express purpose of preserving the routines on celluloid. Often, an additional if limp framework of a plot supported the comedy itself. These films undoubtedly provide only a flavor of how it was to sit in a theatre and watch a comedian or comedy team walk onto the stage and launch into a pun-filled verbal routine or knockabout slapstick. Just as astronomers and physicists strain to peer back in time to glimpse the faintest remnants of the Big Bang, we can now see only scattered films, or hear scratchy recordings, of the well-honed rhythms, costumes, and physical antics of the vaudeville era's top stars in their original form.

Each of the many vaudeville circuits operated as a network of theatres dotted across the country. The Keith-Albee circuit led in the east. The Orpheum circuit, created by Martin Beck, began in San Francisco (later to take up headquarters in Chicago), and led in the west. Performers contracted with a small-time circuit were not afforded many frills. The theatres were small, pay was low, the three-a-day schedule hectic, and the crowds not always the most genteel. It was a life of constant travel. Vaudevillians were always on the move from city to city, traveling by train, staying in drab hotels and boarding houses, and living out of a suitcase. For many, it was almost enough to break the spirit. A major motivation for not giving up altogether was the persuasive dream of making the jump to the big time circuits, with their palatial, big-city theatres, where the pay was better and the opportunities for still further advancement in show business were within grasp. Still, none of it was possible for a comedian without a quality act, and/or a personality that audiences would remember and want to see more than once.

But who were these vaudevillians among whose ranks young Izzy Leopold was so eager to join?

As for the comedians, a remarkable number of them emerged from the immigrant tenements of large East Coast cities such as Philadelphia, Boston, and especially New York. The rise of vaudeville's stage comedy coincided with the tumultuous years of immigration by millions from Europe. The Jews of Eastern Europe in particular, fleeing either religious persecution, devastating poverty, or both, arrived at Ellis Island and shortly thereafter produced the first generation of American-born Jews who looked to show business as the way to success—and, in surprisingly disproportionate numbers, found it. By the mid-1920s, the overwhelming number of vaudeville's biggest comedy stars had grown up in the Jewish ghettoes. Most comedians, regardless of their own personal heritage, played upon the melting pot that New York and other cities had become, and incorporated ethnic humor into their acts. Moreover, if an act failed as an Irish act, nothing was to keep it from re-appearing a week or two later as a German act. Exaggerated stereotypes of Russian, German, Jewish, Irish, and Italian characters delighted audiences who were either laughing at themselves, or perhaps less kindly, laughing at their neighbors.

The tone of much of the ethnic humor of the time could be vicious, as Henny Youngman, the "King of the One-Liners," wrote in his memoirs. "Looking back from today," he wrote, "you almost can't believe these dialect comics actually were allowed to perform. Believe me, you haven't seen racism or anti-Semitism until you've seen it performed by a comic wearing blackface or a prop nose. And yet these guys were among the most popular of all vaudeville performers."

Izzy's flop with the ethnic act he "borrowed" from Joe Welch demonstrated that his own Jewish heritage wasn't necessarily the best source of comedy inspiration for him. Some famous Jewish acts, such as the Marx Brothers, settled on a much more mainstream approach to ethnic humor. As Groucho explained, "We Marx Brothers never denied our Jewishness. We simply didn't use it. We could have safely fallen back on the Yiddish theater, making secure careers for ourselves. But our act was designed from the start to have a broad appeal. If, because of Chico, a segment of the audience thought we were Italian, let them. Then they could admire my proficiency with a German accent."

Having learned his lesson as a failed Joe Welch wannabe, Ed swore off including any trace of ethnic humor in his comedy (years later, a curious observation in a review noted that he was "almost the only Jewish vaudeville comedian who refrains from capitalizing his race"). It's worth noting, however, that there were other popular Jewish comedians of the time, such as Jack Benny and George Burns, who did likewise.

"When I first went on the stage," Ed later recalled, "every dialect in the world was used to make people laugh. People were permitted to call Italians wops, Irishmen micks, Jews hebes—kikes even—they cracked jokes about colored people, funny jokes, very funny, racially funny. I never told dialect jokes. I never told a risque joke in my life onstage. I never offended anyone. I was my own censor for those things."

Comedy legend Fred Allen neatly summed up the vaudeville experience and the possibilities it afforded aspiring performers. "You could be ignorant and be a star," he explained. "You could be a moron and be wealthy. The elements that went to make up vaudeville were combed from the jungles, the four corners of the world, the intelligensia and the subnormal…Vaudeville asked only that you own an animal or an instrument, or have a minimum of talent or a maximum of nerve. With these dubious assets vaudeville offered fame and riches. It was up to you."

Upon the inauspicious end to the Thurber-Nasher repertory company, Izzy held tight to his dream, working out bits of comedy and writing sketches to relieve his boredom selling ladies hats. All the while, Joseph continued to bicker with his son, forever frustrated with the boy's stubborn determination to devote his life to show business. Seeing his hold over Izzy becoming ever weaker, he reportedly tried a dose of psychological pressure, by changing the name of the family business from J. Leopold & Company to J. Leopold and Son (although the "Son" may have actually referred to older brother Leon).

Joseph's final strategy was to invoke the concept of shame. Entertainers at the time, i.e. vaudeville performers, and *especially* comedians, were deemed undesirable individuals in most social circles. "With an actor in the family, how should we hold up our heads?" Joseph demanded. "Think of the disgrace you could bring on us!"

"Okay," Izzy said, "so I'll change my name."

Joseph, taken aback by the idea, considered for a moment. "You can't do that,' he said. "If you make a hit, nobody will know you're my son!" (Years later, Ed said of this exchange, "I never credited my father with a sense of humor, but I think that was one of the funniest things I've ever heard, and the years have made it more so"). As a compromise to keep his identity shaded, Izzy took his middle name, Edwin, and divided it in two, tweaked it a bit, and created the name Ed Wynn. From that point on, he would make no more compromises with his father. Now that he had a stage name, it was time to get back on the stage.

Chapter 2: The Rising Star

> *"Should you ever hear an old-time vaudevillian talk about the 'wonderful, golden day of one-night stands,' buy him another drink, but don't believe a word he's saying. He's lying through his teeth."*
>
> —Harpo Marx

With a new name, but little more than raw talent and grim determination at his disposal to make himself a successful comedian, young Ed Wynn knew he also needed to have some original material ready to present to a theatre manager or booking agent, should the opportunity arise. So, he wrote his own comedy sketch, a dialogue between two college students, called "The Freshman and the Sophomore." Once he wrote it, however, he wasn't quite sure what to do with it. But at least it was something to have in his pocket, if he happened to cross paths with someone who needed a partner.

If a comedian wasn't actually born in New York during the early vaudeville era, breaking into show business there was still the goal. And theatre managers, needing to meet the demands of filling a bill were, by today's standards, quite generous in giving unknown performers a shot at the big time. Ed was now ready to leave home again. But this time he did so with a new dose of confidence. He bid his family adieu and took the hour-long train trip to New York, determined to plant himself there and look for work as long as necessary. Minnie looked out for her son by sending a steady flow of money his way, quietly defying Joseph's blustery objections.

As part of his search for a show business opportunity, one night Ed stopped into a Times Square rathskeller named Kid McCoy's. At the piano were some young, aspiring performers playing and singing. One of them was Jack Lewis, who liked Ed, especially after sizing him up as someone with a bit of cash at his disposal. The two men decided to team up and make themselves known as the Rah Rah Boys, performing "The Freshman and the Sophomore." Ed played the comic, dressed in collegiate garb, while Lewis assumed the straight man duties. A sample bit of dialogue:

STRAIGHT MAN: Why don't you pay a little attention to me?

COMIC: Why I am paying as little attention as possible.

STRAIGHT MAN: You don't get the drift of my conversation. Haven't you decided upon some particular study? For instance, do you like botany?

COMIC: I never met the woman.

STRAIGHT MAN: Botany, my boy, is a study.

COMIC: So is a woman, and the more you study her the more money it costs you.

After talking their way backstage at a Sunday night show at the 125th St. Theatre, they amused manager Elmer Rogers enough to secure themselves a spot on the bill, and got booked on the Percy Williams Circuit (an affiliate of the Keith Circuit) for two hundred dollars a week. The next ninety-eight of those weeks saw them covering a good deal of the country.

"We revolutionized the two-man comedy act," Ed boasted years later. "Up to then the straight man used to swat his partner with a bladder or rolled up newspaper after every joke and chase him around the stage. We stood still and cut out the swatting."

They spent the next two years traveling everywhere, from Montreal to Atlanta. No matter where Ed found himself, he was always sure to mail a picture postcard home from each town on the itinerary, commenting on the scene depicted on the card, adding a few words about life on the road, and signing it "Sonny Ed."

He was doing what he loved to do (on one postcard from Buffalo he reported with pride, "We took five bows, and that's going some"). But even with the team's success, Ed also continued to perform—and improve—as a solo performer for the next few years. As he gained confidence in his abilities as a comedian, their appearances as a duo became more sporadic, and Ed began to look forward to eventually breaking away from Lewis permanently. But they were still appearing together into 1909 before going their separate ways—and none too soon for Ed, judging by a postcard sent to the family that August. "I never felt better since I have been on the road," he wrote, "To think that I won't have to put up with Jack next season. Ed."

Ed stepped up the intensity of his self-education in the field of comedy. He was a student and a collector of jokes, hats, costumes, anything and everything that he might be able to use onstage to get a laugh (over the next several decades, he would accumulate enough props and costumes to fill eighteen steamer trunks). He also began to hone his talent for songwriting. He would go on to write over one hundred compositions—some co-written with others—that would see their way to sheet music publication, the majority of them from his self-produced Broadway revues.

But as of late 1908, Ed was still experimenting to create a stage persona for himself, one that an audience would not confuse with any other comedian they might see onstage. This was a matter of survival at a time when there was a veritable population explosion of comedians and clowns, both good and bad, in vaudeville. Some were content to achieve just enough success to maintain a steady income from one week to the next. Others, like Ed, set their sights much higher.

Groucho Marx wrote, "I believe all comedians arrive by trial and error. This was certainly true in the old days of vaudeville, and I'm sure it's true today…If the comic was inventive, he would gradually discard the stolen jokes and the ones that died and try out some of his own. In time, if he was any good, he would emerge from the routine character he had started with and evolve into a distinct personality of his own. This has been my experience…and I believe this has been true of most of the other comedians."

This was most certainly true of Ed, who, though he was still growing as a comedian, hadn't found his own distinct on-stage personality just yet.

The autumn of 1908 brought a new opportunity for him. Irvin S. Cobb, a successful young journalist and highly-paid staff writer for the Hearst newspapers, wrote a one-act musical comedy with Ed in mind, called *Mr. Busybody*. "I paid Cobb a hundred dollars for it, outright," he said. "Imagine that! Still, in those days, a hundred dollars seemed like a lot of money to both of us."

Described at the time as an elaborate half-hour show, the action in *Mr. Busybody* takes place in a dry goods store, as eight attractive sales girls kill time singing and dancing until Ed arrives to enliven the proceedings still further. He sings the show's title song, and introduces the audience to a different "partner" of sorts, his eccentric Panama hat. Oversized, floppy, and apparently one of a kind, Ed could fold it into two dozen shapes while delivering his daffy verbal shtick.

As of early November, Ed kept a busy schedule, still appearing with Lewis just as *Mr. Busybody* previewed at the Metropolis Theatre in Greenpoint, Brooklyn. The production then moved across the river for its premiere at the Colonial Theatre in Manhattan on November 3. True to form, Ed wasted no time in his efforts to make a name for himself.

"Mr. Wynn…is on the go during the rest of the piece," wrote one reviewer, "finishing the comedy in excellent fashion. His manipulation of a very flexible hat alone is worth the price of admission. He was at his best in a burlesque on the methods of the average salesman, and won dozens of hearty laughs."

The show spent only ten days in New York and then took to the road, *The Philadelphia Inquirer* also singled him out as a bright spot on the bill:

> "Among the novelties probably the greatest success was achieved by Ed Wynn and his company of singers and dancers in a pocket edition of the musical comedy Mr. Busybody. It is one of the liveliest and most entertaining of

the many trifles which have been seen in vaudeville and was given capital presentation. Mr. Wynn is amusing to a high degree and his bunch of agile girls gave him ample support."

The *Syracuse Journal* reported in late January of 1909 that the bill of which Ed was a part positively teemed with talent. It's worth noting that another performer on that same Keith bill was a fellow Philadelphia native "tramp juggler" named William C. Fields, who would become more than a passing acquaintance of Ed's in a few years' time.

"With Ed Wynn and a company of fifteen of the merry-merrys in the chorus line, in *Mr. Busybody*; W.C. Fields, the eccentric juggler with new tricks…There is a boom looked for in vaudeville that will only be exceeded when such other aggregations of talent can be brought together."

Upon returning to New York, Ed even received credit for providing enough comic spark to save an otherwise shaky performance in late February at the Keith & Proctor theatre. One reviewer observed, "Mr. Wynn proved as capably eccentric as ever in his peculiar style of comedy and is still featuring his wonderful comedy hat. He had desperate trouble at times in pulling the act out of its lagging moments, and any great credit in securing the curtain calls received Tuesday night was principally due to his heroic efforts."

Ed was also still performing with Jack Lewis with the Rah Rah Boys act, but the pairing had run its course, and the team finally broke up in early spring. In late May, a dispute of sorts arose between Ed and Lewis, when Lewis claimed he had permission to use the Rah Rah Boys act with his new partner. This came as a surprise to Ed, but negotiations involving a complex exercise in semantics and legalese resulted in Ed voluntarily granting Lewis permission to use the act, rather than have the matter drag through the courts.

By June, Ed had found a new partner, Al Lee, and fashioned a new version of the collegiate act, now known as "The Billiken Freshman." Taking on a new partner so soon after parting ways with Lewis suggests that Ed enjoyed having a partner, as long as it wasn't Lewis himself. *Variety* was happy enough with the new incarnation: "Ed Wynn, with Al Lee, is back in his own act, now called 'The Billiken

Freshman'…A fast and furious talking act it is, however, presented by the pair, and they became the hit of the bill. Wynn is still using his old laugh-catcher, the ever-changeable Panama hat, and has made but few changes in his old act."

The duo traveled through the summer, reaching the west coast in September. They stayed in San Francisco for a month, where *The San Francisco Call* referred to them as "an amusing pair. Wynn personates the swagger, rakish college chap with his fantastic garb, thinking that he is really bad."

They then headed to Los Angeles in mid-October for several weeks' engagement at the Orpheum.

The popularity of Ed's Panama hat inspired him to tinker with the idea of extending his bits of business beyond the hat to other props and novelties. His ever-active comic mind led him to create a few "inventions" to demonstrate to audiences. Some contraptions were little more than visual puns taking physical form, but others offered practical (albeit tongue-in-cheek) solutions to many of life's inconveniences.

The elements of his stage character did not coalesce all at once, but Ed's progress was steady, as was his confidence in his ability to make audiences laugh. "I found that costumes were part of it," he said. "I found that props were part of it. I had some of the greatest props made you ever saw."

Among these early prop inventions was a device for dealing with catching household flies and moths. It was a small folding ladder with the rungs on one side covered with sugar. The flies would collect the sugar as they proceeded up the ladder. Some rungs on the other side of the ladder were removed, causing a sugar-laden fly to lose its footing and drop to its death. The invention generated big laughs with audiences. Ed's follow-up was an idea to prevent moths from eating away at clothes hanging in the closet. A few dozen brass rings thrown onto the closet floor would entice the moths to attack the holes in the rings, leaving the clothes unscathed.

His onstage character was well on his way to becoming a quintessential vaudeville clown: Funny clothes, funny hats, funny props, and a steady stream of puns and corny jokes. But Ed's strongest asset of all was his personal charm, complete with a knowing wink and a chuckle to the audience after delivering an especially bad pun.

Years after he achieved stardom, newspaper stories about Ed's famous size 14 stage shoes offered variations of when he adopted them as part of his costume, and how much the initial investment set him back. One version reported that he bought the shoes in Pittsburgh in 1906 for $3.50. Another said he purchased them in 1909 for $11.00. But Ed did confirm, on several occasions, that he kept that same pair for over thirty years, and estimated the cost of keeping them patched together through all of the wear and tear at between two and three thousand dollars.

With his reputation growing, he began to catch the notice of New York producers as they went about casting their shows. His next big break came with an offer in 1910 by producer A.L. Erlanger to join the cast of *The Deacon and the Lady*, the story of country deacon Flood in the big city. Erlanger even told Ed that he could write his own material—an offer too good to pass up.

At the dress rehearsals for the show (previews began in Baltimore on September 11), Ed stole the spotlight with his antics, much to the dismay of star Harry Kelly, who complained to Erlanger. The insecure Kelly whined that there was too much of Ed in the show, allowing him to dominate the production. It is entirely possible, of course, that Ed was simply too good a performer for Kelly to rival.

Upon hearing of Kelly's complaint to Erlanger, Ed feared that his part was suddenly in danger of being cut—if not entirely, then at least pared down considerably. "There used to be a bar on 48th and Broadway," he explained, "I went there moaning they were going to cut my part. A couple of fellows said here's what you do. At dress rehearsal tonight, play it the way they say. At opening tomorrow, play it the way you want. They won't be able to do anything about it then. I did, and was a great hit."

The Deacon and the Lady opened at the New York Theatre on October 4. Kelly held his own, but Ed emerged as potential star to keep an eye on. As *The New York Times* reported:

> "That the piece gives Harry Kelly an opportunity to appear in his old character of Deacon Flood and Ed Wynne [sic] a chance to exhibit his trained Panama hat, is about the only reason it has for existing. Neither the book nor the music possesses any particular novelty, and were it not for the people

in the company, who are clever in a vaudeville sort of way, the entertainment would be worthy of little more than a mention. Harry Kelly is funny, however, and Ed Wynne made many friends through his appearance in vaudeville..."

Thanks to reviews like this, the New York run lasted only two weeks. The company then hit the road with the show, which was fine with Ed. He hadn't lost his enthusiasm for a life as a traveling vaudevillian. He wrote home from Danbury, Connecticut two weeks into the tour to report, "This is great fun for awhile, a new town each day. Ed."

He closed out the year with yet another new partner, an English comedian named P. O'Malley Jennings, who, like Al Lee, had the experience and know-how to keep pace with Ed's antics. In December, they were on a bill in New York at Hammerstein's. A newspaper ad on December 10 has Ed listed fifth on the bill as "Ed Wynn and Company," rather than using a more conventional "Wynn and Jennings." This choice by Ed constituted a breach of vaudeville etiquette, but by this time he felt his steady stream of partners was keeping the name Ed Wynn from becoming standardized. He wanted audiences to know he was the one and only Ed Wynn, regardless of whoever his onstage partner might be at any given time.

Variety reported of the team: "The turn the two present is of the regulation talking and singing variety...The men dress in evening attire, worn effectively. Large laughs are obtained from the Panama comedy hat worn by Wynn. Jennings makes an excellent foil as an asinine Englishman. At the Hammersteins this week...the act provoked much laughter. It is a clever comedy turn worked out along familiar lines."

ELSEWHERE IN THE COMEDY WORLD, CIRCA 1910

What else was happening in comedy just as Ed found himself on the cusp of stardom? Quite a lot. Here are a few examples:

While it was not considered especially significant at the time, England's Fred Karno comedy troupe arrived for its U.S. tour in the autumn of 1910. Among the troupe members, however, were aspiring performers named Charlie Chaplin and Stan Laurel. During the troupe's New York performance of "A Night In An English Music Hall," comedy film director Mack Sennett, seated in the audience, found himself especially impressed with Chaplin, and made a mental note of his skills.

Chaplin also caught the eye of a certain contemporary and future friend, Groucho Marx: "We were playing in Canada, and so was Chaplin....I took a walk and I passed this dump theatre, the Sullivan-Considine. I heard the most tremendous roar of laughter, and I paid my ten cents and went in and there was a little guy on the stage, and he was walking around kinda funny. It was Chaplin. It was the greatest act I'd ever seen. All pantomime...I went back to the hotel and told my brothers what a real comedian was."

At the time, the young Marx Brothers were themselves traveling with their schoolroom act, "Fun In Hi Skule." Such acts were common on the circuits—the most famous troupe being Gus Edwards'—as they enabled performers to engage in the kind of snappy question-and-answer jokes that were so popular in vaudeville. The schoolroom setting allowed for a lot of physical humor as well. The "students" were usually stereotypical ethnic characters, providing nothing but grief for the teacher. Groucho played a German school teacher in the brothers' early act (Chico's Italian character survived on film as a remnant of this era). The brothers were so full of energy and boasted such a complete arsenal of both verbal and visual comedy as to genuinely intimidate performers who appeared on the same bill with them.

It was also at this time when the first real star of American comedy films emerged, but who, sadly, has long since been forgotten. His name was John Bunny. By the time the rotund, red-faced Bunny made his first film, he had already been a performer in vaudeville and in musical comedies for the previous quarter-century. However, he was one of the first stage comedians to see the potential of film. In 1910, for a salary of $40.00 a week, he starred in *Jack Fat and Jim Slim at Coney Island*, an immediate success. On film, his character became a forerunner to W.C. Fields' later portrayals of the henpecked husband struggling to enjoy a few favorite recreational vices behind the wife's back.

Bunny became an international star and one of the most famous faces in the world. He was mobbed by fans wherever he traveled throughout the U.S. and Europe, and was much admired by his comedy peers. By 1913, he was making a tidy $1,000 a week. Unfortunately, he died suddenly in 1915 at the age of 52, and at the height of his fame. The further tragedy is that very few of his films have survived, and Bunny's contributions to the art form have unjustly been forgotten by all but the most devoted of film scholars.

Chapter 3:
Hitting the Big Time

> *"Eddie Cantor keeps talking about Flo (Ziegfeld). It's 'Flo' this and 'Flo and I' that. Cantor never called him anything but Mr. Ziegfeld. I called him Flo. But only after he was dead."*
>
> —Ed Wynn

In the spring of 1912, as Ed's travels took him to Canada, the Titanic suffered a chance meeting with an iceberg in the north Atlantic. At the Orpheum Theatre in Winnipeg, Ed had a considerably more fortuitous chance meeting of his own, with a young actress named Hilda Keenan. Hilda was part of the same bill as a cast member in a one-act play by Oliver White, called *Man to Man*, starring the respected dramatic actor Frank Keenan and his company. Hilda began her stage career at the age of fifteen, later graduated from Wellseley College, and began touring with her father, appearing in various one-act plays on the vaudeville circuits.

By now Ed's onstage partner was an English comic named Edmond Russon. The tour was a professional success for everyone in their respective appearances. During the stop in San Francisco, the *San Francisco Call* reported that "Keenan has raised 'Man to Man' to the position of a classic by his performance of the role of the downcast laborer, educated, virile and honest, but crushed in spirit." In the same review, Ed was praised as being "one of the best comedians in vaudeville, and his portrayal of an exaggerated type of college boy is clever and diverting."

During the tour, Hilda and Ed began a romance ("She's the cutest thing in girls I ever saw," he proclaimed to anyone who would lend an ear), but their blossoming relationship did not please the elder Keenan in the least. Firstly, the rather pompous actor fancied himself a thespian of high rank and integrity, and took himself perhaps more seriously than was justified—especially since his drinking habit often got the better of him. Ed was, in Keenan's eyes, nothing more than a lowly comedian. Secondly, Ed was a Jew, and Keenan wasn't shy about expressing his prejudices. But his objections could not dissuade either Ed or Hilda from pursuing their relationship. Their divergent travels separated them for long periods, but they stayed in close touch, determined to keep their romance alive. Their paths occasionally intersected on the circuit, and it was during a rare private conversation between Ed and the elder Keenan that the two made an uneasy truce.

Ed's career continued its rapid upward trajectory, so much so that he won a place on the bill for the much-anticipated grand opening of Benjamin Franklin Keith's Palace Theatre in New York's Times Square on March 24, 1913.

When a performer originally scheduled to appear on the opening night bill failed to live up to expectations, Ed received an offer to take the spot (one unconfirmed version of the story places him in Chicago at the time, necessitating a hasty train trip to New York).

Despite the short notice, Ed arrived prepared with a sketch he had written and had been performing called "The Court Jester," in which he played a jester determined to make his morose king (Frank Wunderlee) laugh, risking his own execution if he failed to do so. *Variety* described the fourteen-minute sketch as "a series of jokes (the lady in front knew them all) told the king by the jester. If the king doesn't laugh, the jester dies. The audience wasn't the king. Finally Wynn plays ragtime on the piano. The king laughed and so did the audience (Ed can't play). Finis. Small time speed."

Variety's lukewarm assessment of Ed was almost kind, compared with how the review assessed the rest of the evening's entertainment: "Whoever arranged the opening program for the Palace presented the poorest big-time vaudeville show New York has ever seen."

Ed has often been credited for assuming the role of de facto Master of Ceremonies on opening night. George Burns wrote, "Wynn was so popular, that when the great Palace Theatre opened in 1913, he served as host, introducing acts on the bill and taking part in several of them—making Ed Wynn the first master of ceremonies in show business history." However, Burns was not present on that evening, and newspaper accounts of the time do not specifically describe Ed as emcee. His own recollection of his Palace gig sets the record considerably straighter:

"[Vaudeville] used to announce acts by a boy coming out on the side of the stage and changing cards. But at the Palace they substituted an electric indicator to give the numbers [of the acts]. They had to do this because the acts kept being shifted about on the program. On Thursday of the opening week, the indicator went bad. I said never mind, that I'd just go out there and announce instead. By Saturday, I was doing jokes along with the announcements."

Despite the drubbing the premiere show received in the press, Ed was proudly able to add his stint at the Palace to his growing resume. He had even adapted a more effective ending to "The King's Jester" sketch, by way of a comment from another performer on the bill. Singer Lulu McConnell, of the act McConnell and Simpson, suggested, "Why don't you tell him a dirty joke?" Ed, who never used off-color material in his act, was tempted to do so. After a good deal of consideration, he decided against it, but came up with a variation. At the end of the sketch, in one final attempt to make the king laugh, Ed whispered something in the monarch's ear. The king let out a boisterous laugh, prompting Ed to retort, "Why didn't you tell me you wanted to hear that kind of story?"

The Palace became known as more than just another vaudeville theatre, not only due to the Keith-Albee reputation as a class operation, but also to the theatre's elaborate decor and physical location, on Broadway and 47th Street, right in the heart of the city's theatre district. Its stature steadily grew as vaudeville's premiere showplace, representing the pinnacle of big-time variety entertainment. It brought the performers who stepped upon its stage one heartbeat closer to the "legitimate" theatre, both physically and symbolically. And any performer who could say he or she played the Palace was to be treated in New York, and elsewhere, as an honored citizen of vaudeville. In addition, a certain master impresario of the era kept an eye on the comings and goings of the performers there. His name was Florenz Ziegfeld, creator and producer of the legendary Ziegfeld *Follies*.

The first *Follies* revue debuted on June 1, 1907, with the emphasis on pure showmanship and presenting a dazzling feast for the eyes. Unlike a big-time vaudeville show, the revue featured a regular cast and the same program each night, with perhaps a thin theme running through at least part of the evening of songs, dances, sketches and monologues. The Amsterdam Theatre on 42nd Street became the *Follies'* permanent home. There the stage held magnificent sets adorned with chorus girls wearing costumes so elaborate as to almost obscure the girls themselves (at other times they would appear scantily clad and even topless, but the overall presentation was not designed to appeal to the audience's more prurient interests).

Ziegfeld has been long credited for his uncanny way of spotting talent and loading his productions with the top performers who trodded the boards of the Palace stage. In truth, many of the performers who achieved stardom with the *Follies* were in fact found by Ziefeld's trusty talent scout, Gene Buck, who would present his discoveries to his boss for ultimate approval or rejection. At least one new major talent seemed to arrive on the *Follies'* stage every year like clockwork. For comedians, the revue was a definite a step up from vaudeville, even big-time vaudeville, while falling just shy of most stage performers' ultimate dream, starring in a full-fledged Broadway production. Ziegfeld himself didn't care much for comedians as a species, but knew that his show would be woefully incomplete without them. To his credit, he succeeded in bringing the very best comedians in the business into his fold for thirty years. His first major find was a young female singer-dancer-comedian, barely nineteen years old, but who had been making a name for herself in smaller burlesque revues around New York. She delivered her comedy with an exaggerated Yiddish accent (although she did not speak Yiddish) and had a gift for making contorted facial expressions. Ziegfeld invited the girl, named Fanny Brice, to join the *Follies* in 1910.

The *Follies* also saw the arrival of two extraordinary visual comedians, Leon Erroll and Bert Williams. Erroll, from Australia, was best known for his popular drunk act in which he managed to make his legs as wobbly as rubber. Williams, the first black star of the *Follies*, was one of the most revered comic geniuses of the early twentieth century, but who is, unfortunately, largely forgotten now. The lasting impression he made on audiences, as well as with his fellow performers, has rarely been matched by any of his successors. He wrote and sang his own songs, danced up a storm, and performed a wildly popular and hilarious solo pantomime of a poker game (which, thankfully, has been preserved on film). He often teamed with Errol in the *Follies*, where they performed a number of semi-improvised sketches together.

Ziegfeld, not one to sit on his laurels, continued to add promising comedians to his roster. When he heard from Gene Buck that Ed was one of the few highlights in that first Palace bill, he asked the twenty-five year old clown to join the *Follies*—provided he leave his famous Panama hat behind (Ziegfeld simply hated the hat). Ed agreed, and signed with the show for its next season, which would begin in June of 1914. In the meantime, he continued his travels on the vaudeville circuit performing the new and improved version of "The King's Jester."

Ed was immensely proud that Ziegfeld had hired him as one of the stars in the entertainment world's most prestigious show. But he also had a superstitious streak that he would, at times, indulge to extremes. It manifested itself upon his inaugural performance with the *Follies* on June 1, 1914. He decided that the undershirt he wore on his opening night with the show was indeed his *lucky* undershirt. "That was my first starring vehicle, and I figure that undershirt was good luck," he explained. "It's never been washed, and it's kept under lock and key, but I've never opened a show since that I didn't have it on." His Panama hat may have been exiled to his steamer trunk, but his other elaborate props continued to make their way onstage.

"I played a couple of musical instruments," he explained. "I'd take out a violin right in the middle of the show and start playing *Listen To The Mocking Bird* and then press a button and a little bird would come out of the violin…crazy things like this…what you would call a 'clown' today."

The *Follies* show ended its summer run in the first week of September, with its 112th performance. Ed, having received a steady income in the most prestigious show in the business, felt it was a good time to make things official with Hilda. They married in a civil ceremony on September 4.

The next *Follies* edition opened on June 21, 1915 with the addition of journeyman W.C. Fields, had spent the previous fifteen years traveling the U.S. and the world—from Europe to Australia to South Africa—billed as the world's greatest "tramp juggler." His act, while visually dazzling, was virtually all pantomime. According to Ed, Gene Buck brought Fields to Ziegfeld, who initially rejected Fields for being "an act." Ziegfeld had accepted Ed into the *Follies* the previous year because Ed integrated his material into the overall production. But Fields had a more self-contained act, consisting of juggling and trick gags performed on a pool table. Ed encouraged Ziegfeld to hire him. And, since Ziegfeld liked Ed (as much as Ziegfeld could bring himself to like *any* comedian), he agreed to hire Fields at a salary of six hundred dollars a week, making Fields the highest-paid juggler in the world. But Fields himself was on the cusp of his fateful decision to include his own brand of verbal humor in his act—and eventually retire his juggling act altogether—as his transformation into his now-familiar comic persona continued to take shape. "As a juggler I have nothing more to prove," he wrote at the time. "It's time I try something else."

Ed, on the other hand, claimed that it was *he* who pushed Fields to add verbal comedy to his act. "In the early days of vaudeville, almost all the funniest acts were the acrobats, who were so funny, and the Chaplins, and these kind of people. All pantomime. William C. Fields—the funniest man you ever saw in your life, never opened his mouth. I made him talk for the first time, you know, that was in the *Follies* of '15."

Ed volunteered to write a sketch that would help incorporate Fields' spot into the overall continuity of the show. In it, he could assist Fields onstage as well. Fields was ten years Ed's senior, and as proud a comic performer as any who has ever lived. He worked tirelessly on his juggling, billiard, and pantomime skills, taking his comedy extremely seriously. Ed was the same. Both men took the finest aspects of the clown tradition—comic hats, costumes, exaggerated facial features, an underdog quality, and honed their respective versions of the clown as few of their contemporaries had achieved. And, while they first crossed paths on the Keith circuit, even appearing on the same bill at times, they had never performed onstage together. Now that they were both part of the *Follies*, they also demonstrated how two strong comic personalities in the same show could either complement each other—as Bert Williams and Leon Errol did—or create the opposite effect, as evidenced in a legendary incident described by Groucho Marx.

"[Fields] was a tough guy," Groucho said as a preface to the story. In the pool table sketch, Fields performed trick shots and other gags, while Ed was supposed to look on from the side. But, as was his wont, Ed often gave into his scene-stealing habit, and made funny faces to the audience, unbeknownst to Fields. As Groucho explained, "One day Fields caught him doing this and when Wynn stuck his head out from under the table, Fields was standing there with a pool cue and he hit Wynn on the head and knocked him unconscious. He was a funny guy, but he didn't want anybody to interfere with his act. Or to upstage him."

Groucho's account was not merely the recitation of some invented show-biz myth passed on through the generations. In a letter from Fields to Ed nearly twenty-five years after the incident in question (and long after they had reconciled), Fields wrote, "I sincerely hope you never suffer any more physical or mental pain than you did the night of the bloodthirsty encounter with a pool cue in 'fifteen. Did your head ever heal up?"

Ed had his own version of events. Their sketch worked first in Atlantic City, and then in New York for sixteen weeks, before the show continued on to Boston. It was there that Fields read a review describing the act as the "Ed Wynn poolroom scene, in which he was ably assisted by William C. Fields." According to Ed, Fields somehow held him responsible for the critic's perception of who "owned" the scene, which resulted in an angry Fields punching Ed in the jaw, not hitting him on the head with a cue stick. Yet another version has Fields throttling Ed backstage after the show, but sparing his face from any unsightly injuries, out of professional courtesy. The true chain of events may lie somewhere among the differing versions.

Whichever manner of physical assault was employed, Fields didn't speak to Ed for the next four years.

For his own solo contribution to the *Follies* show—one that was considerably safer than stealing laughs from Fields—Ed devised a sketch that would be ingenious even if performed today.

His piece had him "directing" a film of the *Follies* show. He stood in the left aisle of the theatre near the orchestra pit, as the actors in the film appeared to be following his directions as he called out to them.

The New York Times review of the show offers a flavor of what it was like to spend an evening watching so many expert comedy practitioners—on their way to becoming legends—on one stage in one evening, nearly a century ago:

> "You should see the motion-picture rehearsal with the movie actors—Bernard Granville, Mae Murray, Leon Errol, and all—bobbing about on the screen while Ed Wynn hoarsely directs them from out front…You should see Bert Williams as a West Indian apartment house hallboy. There is a good deal of fun, too, in the mean skit on the midnight cabaret, with the girls rehearsing all the new lyrics written by the chef, and more fun in the antics of W.C. Fields, an expert juggler with a sense of humor, who comes from the halls of the two-a-day."

The *Follies* of 1915 ran for 104 performances, ending on September 18. While Fields and the others stayed with Ziegfeld, Ed decided to move on after his two-year stint. Having established himself as an audience favorite, he joined Ziegfeld's rivals, the Shuberts, for their production of *The Passing Show of 1916*. And, with Hilda expecting their baby, Ed was happy and full of confidence. The production opened on June 22. One review reported, "*The Passing Show* leans on [Wynn] rather heavily and some of this humor takes a good deal of time in passing a given point, but his pseudo-impromptu prattle is always entertaining, and any revue is the better for his hanging around. He received a cordial greeting last evening when he was first discovered sitting in a box and shouting out, 'This show's terrible.' Much of the applause that followed this remark was no doubt a personal tribute…"

On July 27, while Ed was performing a Saturday matinee, word came that he was the father of a son, Keenan. In his excitement, Ed

Ed, doing what he did best, in *The Passing Show* (1916).

couldn't help but interrupt his own performance to announce it to the audience, resulting in a rousing ovation.

But while he missed being present at Keenan's birth, he also missed the physical and emotional torment Hilda endured to have the baby. According to Keenan, she had long expressed a deep-seated anxiety over the pain accompanying childbirth, and, unfortunately, the experience proved every bit as traumatic as she had feared—both for her as well as for the attending nurses. She vowed to herself that she would never repeat the ordeal. Keenan was to be an only child. And Hilda, determined that there be no mistaking in which faith her son would be raised, had him christened Francis Xavier Aloysius James Jeremiah Keenan Wynn.

Portrait of Ed, 1916.

Ed responded to the arrival of his new son by showering Hilda and the baby with gifts—perhaps an early sign of how he would come to substitute personal expressions of warmth and affection for his family with material goods. Indeed, Hilda's mother Kate impressed upon him that instead of spending money on gifts for his wife, a gesture that would make Hilda truly happy would be to marry in a Catholic ceremony. Ed as an adult had become more of a secular, non-observant Jew, and agreed to the idea in order to keep peace in the family.

Now a bona fide Broadway star, he received a steady stream of offers as a matter of course. He was fast-becoming New York's Comedian-For-Hire, and in doing so spread himself mighty thin. He performed in two other revues in 1918, *Over The Top* and *Doing Our Bit*. In fact, for a period of several weeks, he managed to appear on the stages of both shows virtually simultaneously. He accomplished this by arranging to leave each *Doing Our Bit* performance at the Winter Garden for about an hour, so he could grab a cab and hurry to *Over The Top* at the Nora Bayes Theatre. He'd change clothes in the cab, then make his onstage contributions in several scenes scattered throughout *Over The Top*, and then hurriedly return to *Doing Our Bit* before that show's curtain fell.

As a side note, *Over The Top* included the first Broadway appearance of the young brother-sister dance team of Fred and Adele Astaire.

That autumn, Ed took on a featured role in a comedy called *Sometime*, written by Rita Johnson Young, and produced by Arthur Hammerstein. Ed was not the first actor asked to take the part of Loney Bright, a property man/stage manager/wardrobe master for the play's show-within-a-show.

The original actor hired to play Loney, Herbert Corthell, was dismissed during the show's tryouts in Atlantic City. Ed was approached to play the part just six days before the opening (not unlike his last-minute invitation to join the bill on the Palace Theatre's opening night). He agreed to play Lonely on one condition: he had to be allowed to re-write his entire part and add any gags he considered appropriate. After securing Hammerstein's go-ahead to do so, he spent the next six sleepless nights writing. Part of his revision involved giving Loney a softhearted, almost effeminate bent, lisping lines such as, "What is a man to do in wartime when he can't make both ends meet? Make one end vegetables!" (a pun that's better heard than read).

He explained at the time, "I do not expect people to laugh at a silly line, but the spectacle of a simp having hysterics over a silly line gives a new angle to it all."

One supporting actress in *Sometime* was a twenty-five-year-old ingenue named Mae West. In the story, West's character, Mayme Dean, has trouble re-igniting her romance with her aviator boyfriend just home from the war. She tries playing a vamp to entice him, but fails (quite uncharacteristic for the Mae West audiences would later know in her movie career). However, her storyline inevitably took a back seat to Ed's antics.

The show opened on October 4, to reviews such as this from *The New York Times*: "Hammerstein's latest success is, taking it all in all, the best show he has ever produced while in Ed Wynn, the musical comedy stage certainly has an odd genius. This is the day of the 'nut' comedian, and Mr. Wynn is one of the most engaging 'nuts' in captivity... This is the first time he ever acted a role in a legitimate musical comedy. Hereafter he will do this same thing for a long time to come."

West watched and studied as Ed commanded most of the attention and praise in the early weeks of the show's run. But her frustration grew, as she looked for a means to steal a bit of that attention in order to make a name for herself. "I found I was throwing away all my lines," she said. "So I learned to catch the eye of the audience first—usually with some movement. Everything I do and say is based on rhythm...All I had to do, I discovered, was to wander around the stage like so much bait while the boys kept the audience happy with laughs." She also realized that to upstage Wynn, however briefly, she had to throw off his timing and rhythm. One matinee, during a scene in which she needed to cross the stage behind him, she added a bit of slowly gyrating hip action to her stride, which would become her famous walk. The more deliberate pace of her swagger provided an unexpected distraction from Ed's fast-paced, chattering wisecracks. "The audience forgot the comedians," she said. "They forgot the patter...They just looked." Ed may not have appreciated being upstaged by a virtual unknown (after all, he was accustomed to upstaging others), but West made her point that she was fast becoming a force to be reckoned with.

Ed pulled another moonlighting stint during the *Sometime* run (with permission from Hammerstein) as master of ceremonies for *The Century Midnight Whirl*, a vaudeville revue performed on the Century Theatre's rooftop venue. His contributions to the proceedings were described in one review as "frequently highly amusing."

In early July of 1919, Ed joined *The Schubert Gaieties of 1919*, yet another of New York's many upper echelon revues. It was an elaborate show consisting of singers, dancers, and various other entertainers. Ed was called upon to provide laughs during scene changes and other transitions. He would kick off each performance even before the curtain went up, taking the stage and introducing "Mr. Plot," then quickly dismissing him, saying he is not wanted in the *Gaieties*. "Every time it is necessary to shift the scenery," described a reviewer, "he comes out with his conversation and the audience is in no hurry for the next act."

But just as Ed's career continued to reach new heights, a show of support for his fellow performers nearly brought it all crashing down.

On August 6, the Actors' Equity called the first strike in its history. Among the members' grievances was the fact that actors had no control over the number or duration of unpaid rehearsals they were required to hold for any given show.

Ed was not a member of the Equity, but when the strike was called, he made his allegiance known and joined the fight, giving full-throated support via his impassioned speeches at public rallies for the Equity's cause.

One performer in particular found himself suitably impressed with a speech Ed made at a rally on Broadway. The man was W.C. Fields. Ed recalled that, after four years of estrangement between the two, dating back to the infamous pool cue incident, "he came up and kissed me on both cheeks. We became very good friends again."

Ed explained at the time of the strike that his own motives were simple. "I have nothing to gain in this fight," he told a reporter, "but it is the principle of the thing that counts with me." On August 11, he hosted an elaborate dinner at his home for nearly forty well-known Broadway actors, during which they bonded further with their resolve to flex their collective negotiating muscle.

Frank Keenan, himself feeling passionate about the cause, looked upon Ed's involvement in the strike with a newly-open heart. In the form of a rather backhanded compliment, he announced, "At last I am proud of my Jewish son-in-law."

The strike was settled on September 7. Shortly thereafter, The Actor's Equity expressed its appreciation of Ed's involvement by presenting him the Scroll of Honor from the Lambs Club and Equity, signed by 1,800 members. They also selected him to go to Washington, D.C. to secure the new union's charter from the American Federation of Labor.

The Managers Protective Association also expressed its feelings about Ed's involvement in the strike—by blacklisting him.

Chapter 4:
The Mother of Invention

> *"Personality is an amazing thing. Just why it is that Wynn is funnier than anybody else is difficult to say, but he undoubtedly is."*
> —*Vanity Fair* June, 1920

Once the Schubert organization summarily dismissed Ed from the *Gaieties* for his involvement in the strike, he immediately found himself treated as a pariah by the most powerful theatre producers in New York.

But he wasn't about to allow such a setback to snuff out his skyrocketing career. With no financial backing forthcoming from any sympathetic angels, he had no choice but to reach into his own considerably deep pockets to finance and produce his next show. Out of sheer necessity, he called upon his long list of talents and took it upon himself to write the show, direct it, and even compose original songs for it (he couldn't get any union songwriters to work with him, either). He hired non-union performers, mostly vaudevillians, and even circus performers, to comprise the bill. Ed served as emcee, but worked his way into a few of the acts as well. "My comedy was more or less a monologue all the way through the show," he explained. "I never did situation comedy. I brought out comedy in jokes." He even created bits of business based around whatever costumes he could afford to purchase for a reasonable price. "I remember they had some Japanese costumes, so I sat down and wrote a Japanese number to go with the costumes. Other sets, other numbers."

However, his blacklisting prevented him from renting a theatre for the production. He appeared at the offices of his former boss Ziegfeld eleven days in a row, willing to wait each day until Ziegfeld could allow a few minutes of his time for Ed to pitch his new project. On the twelfth day, Ed was on his way through the lobby of the building to make yet another call on Ziegfeld upstairs, when he ran into a theatre manager named B.C. Whitney. The two

talked, and Whitney, who was a fan of Ed's, and not a member of the Protective Association, listened to the pitch for *Carnival*, and the two agreed to form a partnership on the spot to get the show onstage. Whitney in turn presented the idea to his boss Erlinger, who insisted on a considerable cut in order to secure his blessing.

All of Ed's tireless work on the show paid off. *Ed Wynn's Carnival* opened at the New Amsterdam Theatre on April 5, 1920 (later moving to the Selwyn, to make room for the new *Follies* edition), and was received by a fresh round of raves from the critics. *The New York Times* reported that "Wynn, for all that his mood is generally the same, never palls, and while he holds the stage the fun is as close to continuous as any one man can make it."

The show ran through the summer, closing on August 14, and then went on tour.

While in Detroit, Ed reportedly received an offer to appear on film. Exactly who made the offer, and what the film would be, has been lost to the ages. But the Toledo *Blade*, in a piece titled "Will Ed Wynne's [sic] Nut Comedy go on the Screen?" made a good case against the idea, and in doing so provided an apt description of Ed's most appealing qualities as a stage entertainer:

"Wynn's comedy in his *Carnival* show…is of a kind different from that offered by any other comedian. He gives his audience the joy of a personal acquaintance with him, by addressing them directly and intimately, and by mingling with them at the close of the show. His personal remarks made during the action of the show are the things that lure his followers most of all. This is something he cannot do on the screen."

The *Blade* need not have worried just yet, as Ed would postpone his screen debut for another seven years.

As the 1920s began, so did the Golden Age of sophisticated stage presentations. The more structured extravaganzas, such as George White's *Scandals*, and of course, the *Follies*, were going strong (the *Follies* offering headliners Fanny Brice and W.C. Fields, was dubbed "the best of them all"). Ziegfeld's *Midnight Frolics*, presented on the roof of the Amsterdam Theatre, boasted a line-up that included Will Rogers and Leon Errol.

Ed spent the summer of 1921 participating in another popular revue, *The All Star Idlers of 1921*. But he was still on his own when it came to getting his follow-up to *Carnival* off the ground. The new production, *The Perfect Fool*, began to take shape with its first out of town try-outs in Atlantic City, beginning on Labor Day. After a few shows in Philadelphia, the first of the New York previews began on September 8 at the Garrick Theatre. More tweaking followed, as did a change in venue, leading to the official premiere nearly two months later at the George M. Cohan theatre.

A highlight scene in the show involved Ed taking part in an acrobatic act. While the four real-life acrobats (suspended by invisible wires) all balanced on his shoulders, the teetering and buckling eventually resulted in all of them falling to the floor in a heap of flailing arms and legs. Since all of the performers wore identical costumes, Ed sat up and produced a pin with which he'd poke into as many arms and legs as it took in order to find his own. The yowls from the other acrobats, and eventually from Ed himself as he found his own legs, had his audiences in hysterics.

But even after the performers managed to untangle themselves, Ed's glasses would somehow end up on another acrobat. With Ed unable to see without his glasses, and his colleague unable to see

with them, they both proceeded to stumble around the stage in a panic until order was finally restored.

Critics were already beginning to run out of adjectives in their praise of Ed's talents on stage. The *New York Times* reported on the new show thusly: "Ed Wynn came back to town last night in a revue of his own making...He is even more funny than he was in his carnival of a year ago." Several of his talents were on display, including his mind-reading bit and an acrobatic act that revealed his gymnastic skills as well as his talent for gags. And of course, there was his demonstration of new inventions, such as the tea glass spoon that bends over the glass rim to avoid poking the user in the eye. The review concluded by declaring, "Ed Wynn can do almost anything."

At this time, radio was still a technological work in progress, but was also fast becoming a curiosity to the general public. The first commercial station, KDKA in Pittsburgh, came into existence in 1920, broadcasting at brief and irregular intervals, and to precious few sets of ears. Broadcasters, such as they were, were happy to learn that their signals were reaching anyone at all, and were not much concerned with providing content resembling true entertainment. But radio was, nonetheless, creating quite a buzz (a review of the 1922 *Follies* mentioned that W.C. Fields appeared not only as a juggler, but "with a rather hilarious slapstick travesty on the radio passion of the moment").

WJZ in Newark was conducting experimental broadcasts in 1922, when arrangements were made to have Ed and his full cast and chorus perform *The Perfect Fool* live on the air. (Curiously, about half of the sources on this cite February 19 as the date of the broadcast, while others put the date as June 12). This broadcast was the first musical variety show with a full cast to be broadcast on radio. And, when Ed decided he couldn't tolerate the silence in the studio following each joke, he hurriedly assembled a small audience, consisting of whomever he could find in the building at the time, to sit in on the proceedings and laugh at whatever gags tickled their fancy. But this practice would remain *verboten* on radio for another ten years, as broadcasting executives refused to allow audience laughter to be heard on-air.

In 1923, WEAF in New York began programming a regular schedule, but its airtime was spotty, and the programming primitive.

Chapter 4: The Mother of Invention

All the while, radio technology itself was still being developed and improved upon, as a slow and steady stream of stations began transmitting independently of each other to the modest number of listeners who actually owned a "radio set." This new piece of living room furniture was a toy like no other. It was new, the programs were free, and listeners could enjoy their favorite entertainers, and discover new ones, without leaving the comforts of home.

Radio would continue to become irresistible to both its growing listener-ship, and to its potential roster of popular vaudeville performers. But Ed, despite the groundbreaking nature of the *Perfect Fool* broadcast, was not interested.

One day, while the show was on tour in Vincennes, Indiana, he met a nine-year-old boy selling newspapers on Main Street one afternoon. Ed asked him what people do in town for excitement. Not recognizing Ed, the boy immediately recommended Ed's own show, adding that he'd like to be a comedian as well someday. The boy didn't have enough money to see the show himself, so Ed bought the remainder of the newspapers and made arrangements to let him see the performance that night. The boy raced home to tell his mother, who allowed him to attend the show downtown.

Sitting in the balcony, the boy was astonished to see his new friend appear from behind the curtain as the show's star. At intermission, the boy ran from the balcony to backstage, and almost got thrown out by the stagehands. Ed waved them off so the two could continue their chat.

"How do you like the show?" Ed asked him, and then held him up to see the audience filing back into the theatre. At that moment, the boy fell in love with the idea of being in show business and making people laugh. Ed then advised him, "Well, remember, just do comedy. Always say funny things and do funny things. When you say things, say them funny."

The young boy took Ed's advice as he pursued his own career as a comedian, becoming known to the world as Red Skelton. More than thirty years later, Skelton would find himself with the unlikely opportunity to repeat his idol's words back to him (more about that later).

By late March, a combination of exhaustion and troubling news got the best of Ed. During a stop in Springfield, Illinois, he received word of his father's worsening illness. Joseph Leopold had been suffering from cancer in Landenau Hospital in Philadelphia, and Minnie had also fallen ill from the strain. Ed decided to cancel the rest of the tour, which was to run until May 30, and returned to Philadelphia. Joseph died shortly thereafter, and Ed rented an apartment for Minnie, overlooking the ocean in her beloved Atlantic City.

That same year, with ever-growing fame and considerable fortune at his disposal, Ed decided it was time to reach for a higher rung on the social ladder. He and the family left their house in the Kensington section of Great Neck in favor of a far larger and more opulent mansion, elsewhere in town. He dubbed their new home Wyngate. But Hilda and Keenan did not share his enthusiasm for their new digs, which they considered cold, depressing, and just too big. Keenan's descriptions fall just short of the images of the imposing and joyless castle inhabited by Charles Foster Kane in the classic *Citizen Kane*.

It was not entirely by coincidence that no more than six months after moving in, Hilda's personality began to change—slowly and by degrees, and not for the better. Having given up her acting career, she spent a great deal of her time ambling about the huge mansion and its sprawling property, while a chauffeur or other employee would drive Keenan to and from school each day. Ed was too preoccupied with his professional obligations to see the early warning signs of Hilda's degenerative condition. He had another show to create.

The new production was to be *The Grab Bag*. Ed stuck to his familiar but winning formula of giving the audience what it wanted, i.e. having him—with his stories, puns, costumes, and props—front and center for the majority of the show.

A favorite running gag in the show began with Ed demonstrating a harmonica about an inch long. After accidentally swallowing it, he would reappear onstage several times throughout the rest of the show, occasionally letting out a cough complete with the wheezing sound of a full-sized harmonica, supposedly emanating from his stomach.

The Grab Bag opened at the Globe Theatre on October 6, and once again, word spread of his ability to hold a show together with his bag of comedy tricks. As *The New York Times* reported:

> "The new Ed Wynn revue is, as you might imagine, in all respects an Ed Wynn entertainment...There are not more than half a dozen lines in *The Grab Bag* that are not spoken by Mr. Wynn, and certainly there are not two scenes into which he does not enter—and, entering, dominate. However, there was none to complain about this state of affairs last night at the Globe, for Mr. Wynn is unquestionably among the best of the comedians...No comedian in revue excels him in the art of the seeming impromptu."

With *The Grab Bag*, Ed's efforts on the Globe Theatre stage each night produced their desired results. He had yet another success in his pocket. But back at home in Wyngate, the atmosphere couldn't have provided a sharper contrast. Keenan observed, "My mother grew steadily more remote, more isolated inside herself." Ed, meanwhile, was leading a double life of sorts. "At home he was worried over Hilda," Keenan continued. "At work, he was perfecting the lisp, the simper, the lunatic inventions that were his followers' delight. He had the ability to switch his thinking from reality to his rainbow-colored humor, the way you snap a light on and off."

It is curious how there is no indication from Ed's formative years with his family in Philadelphia that could be seen as a catalyst for his later inability to connect emotionally with his own wife and son. But at Wyngate, showering Hilda and Keenan with riches and an opulent lifestyle seemed to be the only way he knew to communicate with them. Despite Hilda's claims (and those of his subsequent wives) to the contrary, Ed saw himself as having tremendous respect for, and impeccable manners in front of women—to which he credited his close relationship with his mother.

Still, Wyngate's expansive emptiness became increasingly unbearable for Hilda. According to Keenan, she grew resentful of Ed's popularity, considering herself both smarter and more talented than he. But, as was the custom for most married women at the time, even those enjoying the lofty heights attained by their show business spouses, she stayed home, half-heartedly socializing among Great Neck's other affluent wives—while her moods grew ever darker, and her drinking increased.

As the Roaring 1920s roared past mid-decade, the fast-growing force of radio continued to entice the American people with the promise of its exciting new form of entertainment.

The date of November 15, 1926 would most likely not ring a bell for the most diehard of entertainment history enthusiasts. But that date did indeed usher in a new era of mass communications, for it was the day (more accurately, the evening) on which NBC officially launched the first radio network in the nation, consisting of twenty-four stations. It did so with a gala event broadcast from several locales across the country, and heard by invited guests via loudspeakers in the grand ballroom of New York's Waldorf-Astoria hotel. The program boasted an eclectic line-up of participants. An opera singer transmitted her performance from Chicago. Weber & Fields performed one of their popular comedy routines. There was also a remote by Will Rogers from Independence, Kansas. Beginning on that night, with the birth of the NBC network, radio became more than a smattering of stations each with a limited broadcast range. And it became more than a fad. Radio became a national obsession.

Most vaudeville comedians whose words were their main stock in trade were eager to seek out whatever open microphones they could find much like Gold Rush prospectors hightailing it to California in search of treasure. But Ed did not embrace radio. He was among the few comedians of his time who felt equally reliant on both visual and verbal comedy for their livelihood. Performing on radio, as he learned from that one broadcast of *The Perfect Fool*, would mean essentially leaving out half of his act. The hats, costumes, props, and funny faces would all be useless on radio. And his reluctance to return to the microphone would hold firm for another six years (until he was made an offer he couldn't refuse).

Back at Wyngate, family tensions saw little relief, prompting Ed to decide that Keenan should be spared bearing witness to his parents' troubles with each other. He made arrangements to send his son to the Harvey School, a private boarding school in Hawthorne, New York.

Hilda's demeanor did show occasional signs of improvement, and even joined Ed on the road during the *Grab Bag* tour, mostly just to get away from Wyngate. She and Keenan had accompanied Ed for both the *Carnival* and *Perfect Fool* tours, so it was a comfortable routine to her. However, when she fell ill again and returned home, she insisted that Keenan return home from school as well. After only six months at the Harvey School, Keenan's semester came to an abrupt end.

There were times when the oppressive atmosphere at Wyngate became so unbearable for Hilda that she would book a five or six-room suite for several days at a time in a top class Manhattan hotel for herself, Keenan, and their servants. Consequently, throughout his childhood and teens, Keenan got to know the hidden corridors, back stairs, and boiler rooms of such mid-town retreats as the Plaza, the Ritz Tower, and the Sherry-Netherland. Upon finally seeing how Wyngate was making his family miserable, Ed sold the house for $400,000, and they returned to their still unsold house in Kensington.

The following year failed to bring much in the way of optimism for the family. Ed's professional successes were growing inversely proportionate to the woes of his personal life. He enrolled Keenan, who was still not yet a teenager, in St. John's Military Academy, as Hilda continued to suffer from bouts of crippling depression. Her husband was totally immersed in the show business life of Broadway, essentially leaving her on her own a great deal of the time. Keenan, by now harboring a growing resentment of his father's emotional and geographic distance, visited Hilda every weekend.

Back in the theatre world, especially in vaudeville, there were also signs of trouble. By the midpoint of the 1920s, the threat came from a double-pronged raid of the public's attention away from the stage, and toward other sources of entertainment.

Motion pictures presented the first perceived threat to the health and well being of vaudeville, and even the legitimate theatre, surprisingly as early as 1908. Two stage actors unions—the Actor's National Protective Union, and the White Rats (an organization of vaudeville actors) expressed their unease with the first signs of movies invading vaudeville theatres. The two unions explored the possibility of merging in order to fight the trend. "The moving picture idea is liable to spread," an Actors Union spokesman warned, "and throw more vaudeville men out of work, and the members of both organizations realize that they must work together for mutual protection." But many visual performers, curious about the nature of film, made the fateful decision to agree to perform their acts, for a fee, before the camera. These filmed versions of their acts became a more desirable commodity for theatre owners than the performers themselves. The films could travel across the country from theatre to theatre, leaving the vaudevillians back home, and in many cases, without work. Theatres that were once homes strictly for vaudeville stage shows began adding motion pictures to their bills. Live stage acts began to suffer from the powerful draw movies held for the public's imagination.

As was his nature, Ed found himself curious about trying a new medium for his comedy. While the reported offer for him to star in one or more films back in 1920 did not materialize, he was certainly not immune to the allure of motion pictures (and the healthy paychecks they offered). In early 1927, the Paramount Famous Lasky Corporation offered him $125,000 to star in his first film, *Rubber Heels*, to be filmed at the Astoria Studios in Queens.

Those involved on the creative end of the picture comprised a promising lineup for the endeavor. The director was a young Victor Heerman, who hadn't had much experience directing features at that point. He would achieve his first claim to fame three years down the road for directing the Marx Brothers in the film version of their stage hit *Animal Crackers* (he would also co-write the screenplay for the 1933 adaptation of *Little Women*). As for the onscreen talent, Ed would be starring with up-and-coming comedy starlet Thelma Todd, who would later feature in two Marx Brothers films, as well as in her own series of Hal Roach shorts with ZaSu Pitts. Silent film comedy and Keystone Kops veteran Chester Conklin— he of the trademark bushy moustache—would also have a part in the comedy. Once the deal was made, Ed got to work on the story, gags, and titles for the film, in which he would star as a private detective.

Then the nightmare began.

To his horror, he quickly discovered that the bulk of his creative input was being rejected by the studio before his ideas ever had a chance to be put on film. In an interview with *Theatre* magazine, he let loose with a barrage of grievances against the producers. "They rejected my titles, most of my story and all of my gags, just because they did not conform with the A B C of motion picture routines. What extravagance!" While he was new to the filmmaking process, he was shocked to see his talents and experience as a comedian virtually discarded in such an offhand manner, and found himself treated like a show business rookie. The film became, in Ed's words, "de-Ed Wynn-ized." To add insult to insult, he was even stripped of his familiar round-framed glasses on camera—the reason given was that wearing them would create the impression that he was imitating Harold Lloyd.

"When I wore the first pair of amber-colored, horn-rimmed glasses seen in the country," he countered, "which had been sent to me from Germany, Harold Lloyd was 8 years old!"

He and Hilda reluctantly watched the film rushes together, and, to no great surprise, were both appalled by what they saw. "I offered the firm every cent they had paid me, if they would kill the picture," Ed said. "It just wasn't I."

At least he had one consolation in the wake of this filmmaking fiasco: Broadway's fortunes continued to smile upon him. In April, he signed with producer George White to star in a new musical comedy, *Manhattan Mary*, for $7,500.00 a week. It was the highest figure ever paid a stage actor at the time. Rehearsals were scheduled to begin at the end of the summer. And, since Paramount wasn't about to destroy all of the existing prints of *Rubber Heels* at his request, Ed decided to leave the country altogether for a few months, rather than have to answer for the film upon its New York premiere on June 11. He booked a trip to Europe for himself and the family. On a personal level, it was high time for the Wynn family to take a real vacation together, before Ed would have to devote most of his waking hours to *Manhattan Mary* rehearsals.

In April, he and Hilda took Keenan out of school for the trip to Europe on S.S. Olympic (hiring a tutor to make sure Keenan continued his studies). Keenan recalled that it was, on the whole, an enjoyable trip for the family, although in his eyes, it served as little more than a band-aid placed over a gaping emotional wound. But even a band-aid, providing some temporary comfort, was better than nothing at all.

Rubber Heels did indeed premiere in June, during Ed's absence, and to so-so reviews. The *New York Times* acknowledged Ed's own disapproval of the final product, and concurred:

> "It is a muddle, this film. To attempt to give an adequate conception of the story would be to ramble on for hours. It is a detective yarn, wherein Mr. Wynn officiates as a Perfect Fool of a sleuth who, despite his irrational actions, emerges triumphant...Mr. Wynn is still abroad. He is not expected to return before July 6 and by that time his Rubber Heels will be cavorting in the distant neighborhood houses, and perhaps in Great Neck, L. I., where Mr. Wynn lives."

The Wynns returned to America in mid-summer, whereupon Ed preferred to look ahead, as he began rehearsals for *Manhattan Mary*.

Shortly after the show began its out of town tryouts in Pittsburgh, Hilda relapsed once again. Ed promptly sent for Keenan to care for her—an errand to which the younger Wynn found himself assigned with increasing frequency, and at his own inconvenience. But the dutiful Keenan did visit Hilda in the hospital, and then returned to St. John's Academy. Once Hilda was discharged, she moved into a penthouse at 3 W. 50th Street. Keenan continued to visit her there on weekends. Ed closed the Kensington house, he had no permanent address, staying in various hotel suites whenever he was in New York between tours.

Manhattan Mary opened on September 26, 1927 at the Apollo Theatre.

In the story, Ed plays Crickets, an aspiring vaudevillian who spends more of his time as a waiter in a cafe than he does onstage. During a clash between two rival gangs, he unintentionally knocks out one of the gang leaders. The rival gang boss shows his appreciation by giving Crickets little choice but to join the gang as their new leader. But as part of the gang's efforts to help the cafe's owner secure her daughter Mary in the starring role in a new Broadway musical, Crickets is assigned the task of kidnapping the show's intended star.

Manhattan Mary's creator and producer, former hoofer George White, gave himself a fair amount of stage time in the show, partly to demonstrate his dancing chops, and, perhaps more significantly, to satiate his own ego.

One of the most famous gags of Ed's career came out of the show. In one of the diner scenes, a gangster tells Ed, "I'm so hungry, I could eat a horse." Ed excuses himself for a moment, returns leading a live horse across the stage to the customer's table, and asks, "Would you like mustard or ketchup?"

The sight gag plus the punchline, and the prolonged, explosive laughter it induced with audiences, became legendary in the annals of Broadway. *Variety* reported the reaction to the joke as "one long scream." Twenty years later, *Life* magazine writer Joel Sayre wrote of the gag, "There are Broadway veterans who still insist that the eat-a-horse joke was the biggest clean laugh within living memory. Anyway it was always at least forty seconds before the audience would let Wynn deliver his next line…"

The *New York Times* reported Ed was in "robustly hilarious form," and described his actions further. "He had modestly effaced himself by unobtrusively leading the orchestra while Mr. White danced, but with the drop of the curtain he was on his way up the aisle, pausing to inquire of the first-nighters what they thought of the show and of himself.

'Wasn't I good?' he was heard to ask one playgoer. There can be no doubt about the answer: Mr. Wynn was great."

Keenan's regular visits to see Hilda brightened her spirits, prompting Ed to arrange another vacation for the family, but one considerably less extravagant than an ocean voyage to Europe. Instead, he took Keenan for a fishing trip in New Jersey, allowing them some rare quality time alone together (although it would be a stretch to call it "bonding," as used in modern-day parlance). It was part of Ed's attempt to spend as much time with his son as possible, since Keenan had already been nursing his anger over his father's on-again, off-again involvement with the family. For the second part of the vacation, Hilda joined them for a trip to Martha's Vineyard.

Keenan then changed schools once again, leaving St. John's Academy and returning to his first home away from home, the Harvey school. As for Hilda, she simply could not seem to maintain her mental balance for any significant stretch of time before succumbing again to churning emotions and alcohol. According to Keenan, she "retained a strong love for [Ed], though she rejected him for what he turned out to be—a distant man who lived for applause. In her sickness, her despair drove her to dreadful things." Sadder still is the possibility that therapy or today's common prescriptive drugs for easing depression symptoms may have alleviated Hilda's condition while still in its early stages.

The situation deteriorated to the point where Ed decided Hilda needed more constant care. By 1929, he found it necessary to make arrangements for two of his relatives, Samuel and Ruth Greenberg, to care for her. Little did he know at the time that the precise nature of their arrangement would become a point of contention in an emotionally harrowing legal showdown a few years later.

Chapter 5:
The Toast of Broadway

"A person is not a success because of what he has to offer the public; success comes as the result of how the public reacts to what is offered."

—Ed Wynn, 1934

In the early days of 1930, Ed joined forces once again with his old boss, Florenz Ziegfeld, to create his new show, *Simple Simon*. It was billed as "a musical extravaganza in two acts and thirteen scenes."

The plot centers on Simon, a Coney Island shopkeeper who sells books and newspapers, but prefers to read only fairy tales because he does not like to read bad news. One day he falls asleep in front of his shop and dreams that his fellow merchants from Ferrymen Alley are fairy-tale characters (Cinderella, King Cole, Jack and Jill, Snow White, etc.) and that he is the hero in each of their fables.

Ed found himself challenged with a balancing act of sorts while writing the show. He wanted to combine the elements of childlike fantasy with more adult (but clean) humor.

"For every hickery-dickery-dock," he said, "there was going to have to be something sort of sophisticated, like a bottle of Scotch." As it turns out, he meant that literally as well as metaphorically; at one point in the show, a horse appears onstage with a flask conveniently secured to its hip (Ed apparently was convinced that bringing a live horse onstage was always good for a big laugh). But, because children as well as adults were encouraged to see the show, he would refrain from smoking his ever-present cigar onstage.

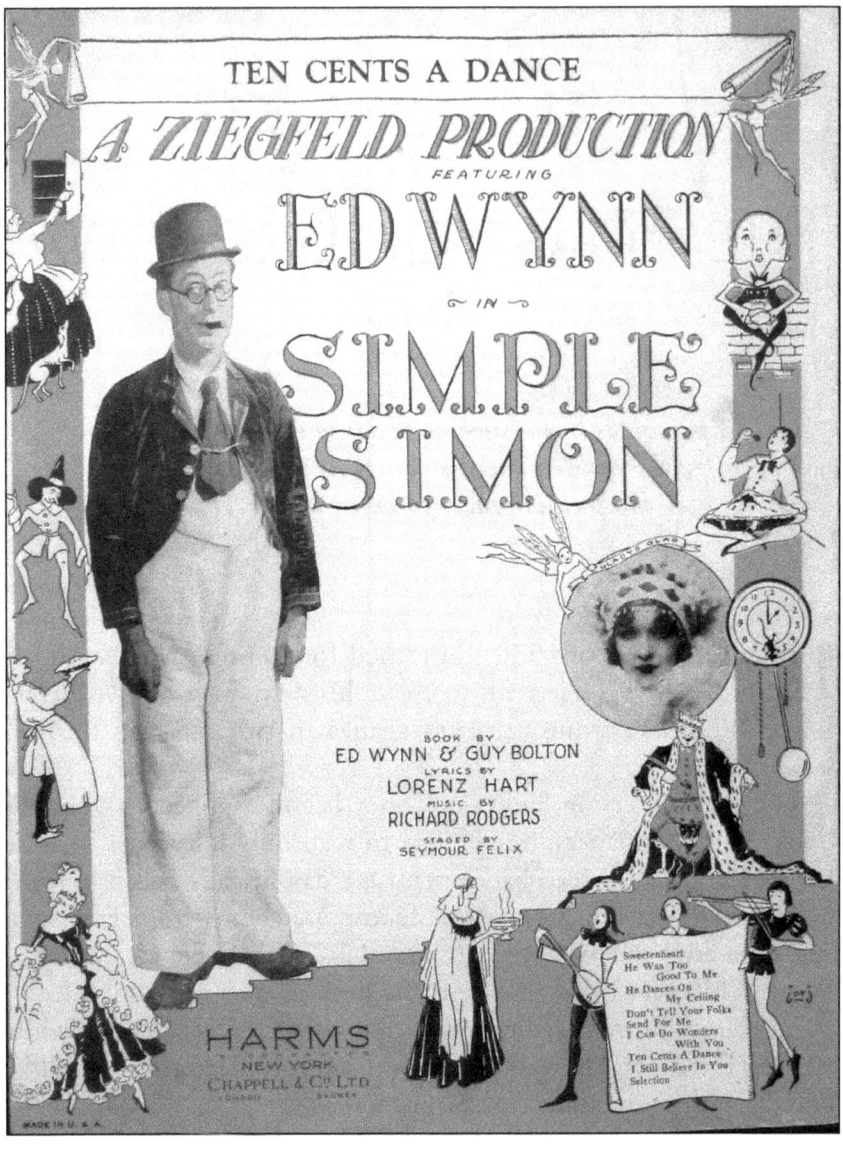

At one point in the writing process, Ed found himself struggling with his own plot twists. Ziegfeld found help from no less a talent than Guy Bolton, a prolific writer of stage plays, novels, and screenplays (he collaborated with the great P.G. Wodehouse on twenty-one shows). Bolton would later write the book for Cole Porter's *Anything Goes*, and, for *Simple Simon*, he helped steer Ed through a creative rough patch in the story.

"With *Simple Simon* I was the only actor-partner Ziegfeld ever had," Ed stated with pride. "I wrote the book, then when I got to the love interest the whole thing got beyond me. I found I was getting engaged to myself. Ziegfeld said to hang on, that he would fix that. He got Guy Bolton to come and unmarry me." The music this time was the product of two legends in the making—Richard Rodgers and Lorenz Hart, although their efforts here did not produce a hit.

The show opened on February 18, to reviews that singled out Ed as the standout reason to pay the admission price. While the flow of the material may have been clunky at times, the production itself provided generous helpings of brightly colored sets, eye-pleasing dancing girls, and costumed characters and creatures to create Ed's fantasy world. He personally received the kind of raves to which he was becoming accustomed. Indeed, few comic performers on the New York stage—or perhaps anywhere else—had as strong and loyal an ally among theatre critics as Ed had in a fellow named Justin Brooks Atkinson, who became *The New York Times* theatre critic in 1925 (using the byline J. Brooks Atkinson). With the arrival of each new Wynn production, Atkinson's reviews overflowed with his love and enthusiasm for Ed's silly but ultimately charming brand of comedy. His review of *Simple Simon* was his first of many such Wynn-inspired raves:

> "...It is Ed Wynn's field day, and quite properly. For amiable and droll and delightful as the Perfect Fool has been in the past, he has never seemed so indisputably great as he does this time in the full ripeness of his art—not merely an expert musical stage comic, although it is essential that he should always be that, but an artist who lifts his tomfoolery into the realms of fantasy...The Perfect Fool has become one of the two or three great comedians of the day."

Simple Simon ran for 135 performances, closing on June 14.

By 1930, sound films were obviously here to stay. The 1930s became the first decade in which comedians, especially verbal comedians, had a genuine choice of three viable forums in which to work: the stage, radio, and films. Many tried their hand at all three.

A surprising number of them found success with all three as well, considering the different demands each medium placed on its performers. This resulted in an extremely busy decade in the comedy world, with performers crisscrossing among all available media as they found their true strengths.

And so it was with Ed. After *Simple Simon* closed shop on Broadway, he ventured back to Paramount's Astoria Studios to take on motion pictures once again, but under very different conditions than those he encountered filming *Rubber Heels*. This time, the picture would be a talkie called *Follow the Leader,* a filmed version of *Manhattan Mary*. And Ed was already familiar with the story and his character, Crickets. He also had the first opportunity to include his verbal gags on film, along with a healthy dose of slapstick (also of interest, in retrospect, is the casting of the two young female leads, Ginger Rogers and Ethel Merman). He also got to repeat the famous "I could eat a horse" gag from the stage show.

The reviews were considerably kinder than those for *Rubber Heels.* "Mr. Wynn is a joy to behold and listen to," wrote *The New York Times*' Mordaunt Hall, "and one's sole regret is that he does not occupy the centre [sic] of the screen often enough during the first half of this production. It is, however, a picture that winds up with a stream of ludicrously humorous turns, which provoked their full quota of mirth from an audience yesterday afternoon. This affable comic with his fund of laughable inventions is another player who benefits distinctly by being heard as well as seen, for it is plain that his gags could never be pictured to such advantage in a silent film."

The film trade magazine *Exhibitors Forum* proclaimed, "For sheer nonsense this piece has few equals unless it is a Marx Brothers' show. Ed Wynn, long known as the 'perfect fool' in musical comedy, continues to hold down his title in *Follow the Leader.*" Despite the encouraging notices for Ed, the film wasn't a commercial success. But he was soon to return to more homey surroundings anyway, on the stage.

In August, he purchased the production, music, and picture rights to *Simple Simon* from Ziegfeld, for an undisclosed sum (the cost of the show's production in Ziegfeld's theatre was reported at $197,000, but Ed did not reveal the production's purchase price).

He spent time making revisions in the show before taking it on a six-month national tour on the Schubert circuit in October. Ed had recently settled his differences with Lee Schubert, with whom he had been on the outs since the Actor's Strike back in 1919.

In March of 1931, *Simple Simon* returned from its tour to reopen in New York for a short run. Two months later, Ed returned to the Palace Theatre for the first time since he helped christen the revered vaudeville venue eighteen years earlier. As a gag, rare for its time, the theatre's program for this production listed Ed's name eight times, each time preceded by the phrase "original master of ceremonies" in a different language. Ed assumed the role of emcee once again for the other acts on the bill, while largely borrowing his own material from *Simple Simon*, to equally positive effect. His new material consisted of extended introductions for each of the acts, which he turned into verbal flights of fancy before getting around to bringing the performers onstage. The *New York Times* raved, "Ed Wynn is still the most winning and likable of the buffoons, a fantastic comedian who, in the business of creating and moving through his own special world of unreality, has no peer in the realm of song-and-dance entertainment."

Within a few months, he was working on a new, original stage production called *The Laugh Parade*. But this time, he and the show suffered a discouraging two-month trek of out-of-town tryouts before heading to Broadway. *The Laugh Parade* found itself playing to largely unimpressed audiences across the country. Ed worked on the book day and night, with assistance from Ed Preble, re-writing nearly everything from the first scene to the last, with little success. It came as somewhat of a mystery how his famous style of combining visual gags with corny puns and asides, which had been so successful in his earlier productions, was suddenly falling flat in *The Laugh Parade*.

An article appearing in *Radio Stars* magazine describes the try-out period in the most dramatic, even desperate of terms, implying that Ed put his very health in danger due to the stress and sleepless nights he spent reworking the production. "With a few loyal helpers," the piece explained, "he rewrote and remade that whole show. Into it he put everything he had learned in thirty years of showmanship…In the end, he found himself carrying almost the whole production.

He was on the stage almost all the time. Soon, weariness was dragging at his muscles and jerking at his nerves, but he worked on."

Despite his dedication to getting things right, opening night was still a near-disaster.

Word that the show had been bombing out of town reached New York, where audiences and some critics stayed clear of the Imperial Theatre. Ed had to buy hundreds of tickets himself and give them away just to secure a full house for the November 2 premiere.

What happened next probably veers closer to myth than to fact, considering how the entertainment journalists of the day were given to embellishing stories about the stars for the sake of dramatic effect (and better magazine sales). During the opening night performance, so the story goes, Ed's mother was in the front row, watching her son struggle for laughs. During one of his monologues, Ed paused to include his mother's often-used "and so-o-o-o" expression that came in handy when pausing before continuing with the story. His voice cracked while doing so, turning it into a high pitched yodel that brought the biggest laugh of the night to that point. It gave the proceedings with a new jolt of energy, and was to become Ed's widely-imitated catchphrase for years to come. Whether the incident unfolded in quite that movie-moment fashion or not, the important thing was that Ed was once again onstage, wearing his typically outlandish outfits, hats several sizes too small, oversized trousers and shoes, the waistcoat, and uttering wonderful nonsense all the while.

By this time, his gag inventions were rivaling Thomas Edison's in number, if not in their potential for official U.S. patents. He treated interviewers to descriptions and demonstrations of the gadgets, speaking tongue-in-cheek, as if they might actually find their way onto retail store shelves someday.

Among the gizmos he was presenting to audiences by this time:

- A silver ring which would fit over the rim of a paper cup to make it sanitary, and thus re-usable.

- An overcoat with sharp, protruding steel spikes to give the wearer ample room on the subway.

- Anti-skid chains applied to shoes, like those put on car tires, to avoid slipping on polished floors.

- An ice tea spoon that folds over the top of the glass, saving the drinker from getting poked in the eye with the end of the utensil.

- A large, sponge cuff, worn the length of the forearm, to soak up dripping butter while eating asparagus.

- For eating a grapefruit—a pair of eyeglasses with mini windshield wipers to protect the eyes from squirting juice.

- Cheese fork with nose guards for slicing pungent varieties such as Limburger.

- A transparent mousetrap with no doors. Food is placed inside to be visible to mice, but with no way of getting to it, they decide to try the house next door.

The Laugh Parade program, signed by Ed.

One of his most celebrated inventions was a device for eating corn on the cob. It consisted of what was, to all appearances, a typewriter carriage that grips the cob at both ends. As the user eats the corn, the carriage moves over automatically, thus presenting new grains to the hungry eater. The same device that moves a piece of paper in a typewriter turns the cob around, making all of it accessible to the diner.

The critics' raves for Ed's productions were by now becoming commonplace. *Time* magazine said, "*The Laugh Parade* goes on its merry way without benefit of libretto or commonsense. At one point particularly does Mr. Wynn...rise to appreciable heights."

This is when he imitates a juggler of the Tony Pastor era, complete with silk tights and handlebar mustache. For incidental music he requests the orchestra to play "something in a jugular vein."

Brooks Atkinson's review of *The Laugh Parade* read, in part:

> "To me Wynn is immune from the law of diminishing returns. Although he is a formula comedian, he has a stage personality of such warmth and disarming simplicity that the repetition of lines, giggles, grimaces, costumes and crack-brained inventions seems hardly to matter at all...The foolish grin, the flabby chin, the arched eyebrows, the solemn spectacles, the witless flutter of hands—well, everyone knows them. It all makes a fantastic invention in the sphere of things that are silly."

Finally, John Mason Brown bestowed upon Ed perhaps the highest compliment any comedian could ever hope to receive. "...While he is at work," Brown wrote, "Mr. Wynn succeeds—as almost no other major comic in our theatre succeeds—in wiping out all recollections of the everyday world outside the theatre and in making the laughter of the moment seem more important than life itself. He is the king of nonsense, and the emperor of idiocy...*The Laugh Parade* is well nigh the perfect Ed Wynn show."

Chapter 6:
The Fire Chief

"I guess the biggest adjustment we all had to make between vaudeville and radio was that in vaudeville seventeen minutes of good material could last for years, while on radio seventeen minutes of good material would last seventeen minutes."
—George Burns

As 1931 turned into 1932, *The Laugh Parade* continued its triumphant run at the Imperial Theatre, where it would become Ed's longest-running self-produced show, totaling 231 performances.

But it was at this very point in Ed's career, when both audiences and critics couldn't seem to get enough of the master clown of the stage, the gap between his professional success and personal heartache continued to widen. There were moments when even his natural abilities to make theatre-goers double over with laughter weren't enough to make him happy. In April, as he prepared for the show in his dressing room, painting on his long, curved, clownish eyebrows, he revealed to a journalist, "If I had to do it all again, I'd never taken up this business, that's all. Being a funny man all your life has just the opposite effect on a man in later years. You keep getting sadder and sadder, and you don't know why."

In Ed's case, there was no real mystery as to why. In the past few years, Hilda had become increasingly vulnerable to fits of the crippling depression, which at times endangered her very sanity. Keenan's feelings toward his absentee father were deteriorating as well. "If his brand of humor or his money could have solved his private problems," he wrote, "everything could have been put right in a second. But our broken-up family life was a humorless mess, and we all took it for granted that Dad's career would continue to pay off in an endless stream of thousand-dollar bills."

As much as Ed would have loved to bring warmth and happiness to his family along with the material luxuries he lavished upon them, it was as if he could only feel his life energy coursing through him when he was onstage. He became a living cliche of the sad clown who laughed for his public audiences but who despaired in his moments alone. This was Ed's life in 1932.

In the early 1970s, Keenan recorded in an introduction for an LP of Ed's radio broadcasts. During his apparently extemporaneous reminiscences, he spoke of his father with a greater compassion, even a wistfulness that was noticeably absent on the pages of his own 1959 book:

> "I would say that my father was a very gentle man, who was put under great stress by everybody. He tried to do the best he could for everyone. He really tried. I think he was a very sad man. Not in the sense of the Pagliacci, but that he said he achieved great success, monumental success, and he would be in a room with the door closed, and say, 'why am I not happy?' I think he had a good life. But I think also that he expended more outside the family, so that when he came home, I would say, "Dad..." "Quiet!" 'cause he was worn out by then. This kind of a thing is very disturbing to him as a performer, and also to those who surround him... But he had expended so much outside—obviously he gave to people—but there was nothing left when he came home."

In the early 1930s, there was no avoiding the runaway momentum of the communications revolution known as radio. For comedians, the idea of reaching a far greater number of ears in one evening than they could in years on the stage, was an intriguing concept, to say the least. The sheer level of exposure to the masses a performer could attain, simply by standing in front of a lone microphone, was staggering. Bob Hope loved the fact that "radio was a medium where, every week, more people would hear my jokes than had seen my vaudeville act in ten years on the Gus Sun Time [vaudeville circuit]." Besides, the money was great. What a perfect new innovation for both the performers and their audiences—or so it seemed.

Once NBC had established its network in 1926, manufacturers of consumer products, from cigarettes to coffee to gasoline, bought chunks of radio air time, on which they could effectively advertise. They then sought the biggest names in show business to star in their own programs, thus ensuring a sizeable audience for some rather long and heavy-handed commercial announcements. But there were still a few skeptics in show business who considered radio a novelty that would soon wear out its welcome. Jack Benny admitted that he initially wondered who would want to hear disembodied voices from a speaker when you could see real entertainers in the flesh on a stage.

The answer was: Everyone. Once radio became a feasible mass medium for broadcasters, and an affordable addition to the American family's living room furniture, it changed the nature of entertainment. It also struck vaudeville at its very heart.

While Benny may have been initially skeptical of radio's drawing power, most of his contemporaries welcomed its obvious perks. Benny's friend Fred Allen, after getting by with mediocre success in vaudeville, saw many popular comedians appearing as guests on radio variety programs, or receiving offers to host their own. The contrast between a life on the stage and one in front of the microphone convinced him to pursue the latter.

"In the theater," Allen reasoned, "the actor had uncertainty, broken promises, constant travel and a gypsy existence. In radio, if you were successful, there was an assured season of work. The show could not close if there was nobody in the balcony. There was no travel and the actor could enjoy a permanent home. There may have been other advantages but I didn't need to know them."

Radio was a fascinating medium full of possibilities, but as every stage comedian soon discovered, it was not a perfect one. Performing on the air proved to be a far more disorienting experience than expected. Even the top comedians of the day quickly proved themselves to be woefully ill prepared for the demands of the seemingly innocuous radio microphone. Sure, the audience for any given performance on radio was measured not in hundreds, but in millions. However, *this* audience was as invisible to the comedian as he was to his listeners at home. Two troubling questions arose: How could a comedian maintain any kind of connection with his audience this way? And just how well would the familiar styles of vaudeville comedy travel over the airwaves?

The issue was one of how a time-honored style and onstage delivery would have to be adapted for a new method of communication. For many, it came as a sort of culture shock. The finest comedians were being invited to appear on programs, often hosted by singers, such as Rudy Vallee and Kate Smith. In those early days, however, comedians were doing little more than reciting their established vaudeville routines by heart. Or, those who tried fresh material could do so only by reading a script in front of a microphone in a silent studio. The dramatic shift in ambience proved so daunting, it became clear that the very nature of comedy itself had to change. Adjustments needed to be made to ensure any comedian's longevity in radio, as broadcast signals sent the very spirit of comedy gliding through the ether. This radio business was going to be tough.

In 1931, Ziegfeld *Follies* and Broadway veteran Eddie Cantor became the first comedy star to be offered his own regular network program. It behooves us to consider the repercussions of Cantor's move to radio, in order to appreciate the creative environment into which Ed would enter the following year.

Cantor, as star of *The Chase and Sanborn Hour*, was the first radio comedian not only to perform in front of a live audience on a regular basis, but the first to encourage the audience to respond audibly while the show was on the air. Imagine sitting in the studio audience of your favorite late-night TV talk show, and being instructed not to laugh out loud at the jokes by the host or the guests for the entire show. As difficult as it may be to fathom now, studio audiences throughout the 1920s were instructed to remain silent for the duration of the programs, and to even suppress their laughter during comedy segments. Performers would stand on a stage facing the audience but with a thick sheet of glass, or "glass curtain," hanging between them. The logic behind this practice remains elusive, but broadcasters at the time apparently felt the distracting sound of audience laughter during a broadcast would confuse, even unnerve, those listening at home.

"Keeping an audience under glass was one thing," George Burns wrote, "but asking them not to react made working in front of them really tough. We would do great material and these people would sit there smiling loudly."

But Cantor's breakthrough of encouraging audience responses on the air didn't occur immediately. During his inaugural 1931 season, and for part of the following year, he lived with the glass curtain just like every other radio performer. Before each broadcast, an announcement from the J. Walter Thompson ad agency (which handled Chase and Sanborn) was read to the studio audience, requesting them to remain quiet.

During one broadcast, however, Cantor and bandleader Jimmy Wallington acted a skit about two women truck drivers. Suddenly, Cantor succumbed to a spontaneous urge and ran down to his wife and Wallington's wife seated in the front row, and grabbed their hats and fur scarves. He and Wallington wore them for the remainder of the skit. "The audience is howling," Cantor recalled in his memoirs, "and there's no stopping them as we two clowns mince around in our finery. They keep on laughing until the show is over." Immediately after the show, a representative from J. Walter Thompson called the wary Cantor, who was expecting a reprimand, and surprised him with praise for enlivening the show with the audience's participation.

Cantor concluded that listeners sitting at home would feel more involved in the proceedings if they heard the studio audience laughter, and thus would feel more inclined to laugh along while listening to the show. It's only fair to note here that, while Ed is usually credited with the innovation, because he was the first to perform in front of a live, laughing audience for the one-time 1922 broadcast of *The Perfect Fool*. But Cantor's trend-setting broadcast took place before *The Fire Chief* show premiered.

Once it became inevitable that the glass curtain's days were numbered, yet another issue came to light. As it was in vaudeville, Cantor's on-air performance was one of constant movement. His detractors sneered that he naively equated perpetual motion with giving a true comedy performance. Ed himself referred to him as "a man with no talent whose idea of entertainment is rolling his eyes and moving his hands in circles." Others, like Fred Allen, were just as disapproving, pointing out how Cantor "wore funny costumes, pummeled his announcer with his fist and frequently kicked his guest star to obtain results."

Milton Berle also concurred, offering a sober assessment of Cantor's almost desperate efforts to keep the laughs coming at any cost: "Eddie Cantor had to fight for his laughs. Unlike some comedians who are ready to garner laughter a minute after birth, Cantor wasn't born a funnyman...He had a desire to be funny, the urge to provoke laughter. The equipment was missing. He wished himself into comedy. Many comedians need writers, but Cantor NEEDED writers." Natural ability or not, Cantor's manic performances burned into the memories of those who simply couldn't take their eyes off him, even when he was supposed to remain stationary behind the microphone stand.

A dilemma arose among comedians like Cantor, who were accustomed to including visual, kinetic gags in their stage performances: they hadn't considered how it would play on radio. They wore costumes, mugged for the studio audience, and insisted on including sight gags to keep the patrons sitting in front of them laughing along, thus eliminating the possibilities of dead air. As true vaudevillians, they needed to hear the laughter—not just for its spiritual uplift, but for its more earthly purpose of helping them with their timing. This in itself was a reasonable argument for allowing audience laughter on the air. However, the practice of throwing in visual bits of business created the risk of alienating radio listeners at home, who would often hear laughter without hearing any joke preceding it—such as during that first frenzied bit as Cantor snatched the hats and scarves. So, while those of Cantor's ilk may have scored points for inviting home listeners to feel more a part of the laugh fest, they were often just as guilty of shutting them out by catering primarily to the live audience. The antics for the benefit of their theatre-goers were obviously lost on the millions at home who had no use for funny faces and slapstick on a radio show.

"To sit by a radio receiver and hear laughter without knowing what provoked it is extremely annoying," grumbled John Carlisle, director of programming for CBS. "So annoying, in fact, that some comedians would do better to work without a studio audience." That was fine with Fred Allen, for one, who also found audience laughter distracting, even when it was coming from his own audience. George Burns joked, "I think Fred Allen didn't even want people listening." But the glass curtain's ship was about to sail, allowing laughter to flow freely through the air, and *on* the air.

As Cantor solidified his radio success, Ed began receiving offers to launch a program of his own. Radio continued raiding Broadway and vaudeville for the biggest stars in the business, going for one big name after another to star in his or her own program. Many of the most successful stage comedians of the time were those who had mastered verbal comedy, with little need for visual gags. Jack Benny, Burns & Allen, Fred Allen, Bob Hope and others were all adept at getting laughs through their words alone, so they were the natural choices to use their talents on radio.

But unlike most of his comedy peers, Ed still wasn't interested in radio. He considered his very existence to be that of the stage performer, and felt he had to be seen to make any mark as a comedian. He wore clownish make-up and costumes, utilized his expressive face, and displayed a trunk-full of gag props. No, Ed didn't want to be on radio.

He wanted to be on television.

There was just one problem with this: Television did not exist in 1932. Strictly speaking, it existed only in its embryonic stages of development, but just the very concept had already begun to stir the public's imagination (an interesting scene in the 1933 W.C. Fields film *International House* features a demonstration of "radioscope," i.e. television, to a group of potential investors). The practical possibility of transmitting images through the air was being explored as early as the mid-1920s, when radio itself was still in its infancy. Occasional newspaper stories about television offered progress reports on the exciting new invention, whose availability to the public was supposedly just around the corner. But radio's technology was by far the easier of the two challenges to refine and master, as television's development lumbered somewhat throughout the 1930s.

Most entertainers paid little heed to television's inevitability in those earliest days of its history, but there were exceptions. Mary Pickford, the world's most famous leading lady of silent films, expressed her enthusiasm about television's potential in a 1934 interview, in which she demonstrated remarkable insight of her own. "Television will revolutionize broadcasting just as the talkies did the silent screen," she predicted. "It may hurt some who are not able to survive when the new medium arrives, but it will smile on many others, just as happened when the talkies supplanted the movies. It is a case of the survival of the fittest, but, in the final analysis, it is for the good of the art."

And then of course, there was Ed, who couldn't keep himself from dreaming of the possibilities. His eagerness, even impatience, to appear on TV reflected how he valued his own talents as a superb visual comedian. A radio audience would only have access to half of his comedy repertoire. He didn't want to shortchange his fans, or himself.

Television's progress was steady, but slow. Experimental transmissions in cities like New York and Chicago reached a few city blocks from one laboratory to another, but there would still be a considerable wait for the small screen's revolution to take hold.

So, with a reluctant acknowledgement that he would have to sit tight for several years before he could appear on the intriguing little screen, Ed half-heartedly listened to the offers to star in his own radio show. In the early spring of 1932, he was still enjoying his successful run in *The Laugh Parade*, and decided on one way to keep the radio executive hounds away: ask for a ridiculously high salary that no one in his right mind would ever agree to pay. After all, he was the toast of Broadway, and could command just about any terms he wanted.

At one point during *The Laugh Parade*'s run, a man attended four different performances of the show in his high-priced box ($5.50), but drew attention to himself by sitting with his back to the stage each time. His intention was to experience the show solely by hearing it, to determine just how funny Ed was without being seen. His final assessment was that Ed was funny even without his costumes, props, and sly facial expressions. This proved to be a turning point in Ed's career, since the rather odd audience member was George W. Vos, chief advertising man for the Texaco company. His experiment convinced him that Ed should star in his own Texaco-sponsored radio program.

Whether it was Vos himself or another Texaco representative who made the initial contact with Ed is unclear. But a company man did visit Ed and asked why he hadn't gone into radio yet. His persistence began to annoy Ed, whose answers failed to discourage the inquiry.

"You couldn't pay me enough money to go on the radio," he said flatly, trying to rid himself of the nuisance.

"Money is no object," was the reply. "How much would you want?"

"That sort of stumped me," Ed later said of the exchange. "I mentioned a price I considered prohibitive. I never thought anyone would pay me $5,000 for a single broadcast. I don't believe any one is worth that much. Imagine my embarrassment when he said that amount would be quite satisfactory."

Considering how this occurred during the depths of the Depression, Ed may very well have been embarrassed by his own salary. But he was adamant with his key demand that he perform the show in make-up and costume, and before a live audience that was permitted to laugh out loud during the broadcast, permanently banishing the glass curtain from the proceedings. To that end, the program would be performed and aired from the New Amsterdam Theatre's new 675-seat rooftop venue, (which began as a roof garden, was later converted into a theatre, and then became the NBC Times Square studio).

The Fire Chief premiered at 9:30 p.m. on Tuesday, April 26. Ed found what would prove to be invaluable on-air assistance in the person of good-natured announcer/straight man Graham McNamee, a popular sportscaster who would, for the next three years, become closely linked with *Fire Chief* in the minds of the nationwide audience. For his stalwart contributions to the show, McNamee received $250.00 a week.

The stage set consisted of a backdrop curtain sporting a huge banner for Fire Chief gasoline. Two large gas pumps flanked each side of the stage. The notorious glass curtain was conspicuous by its absence. Just as Ed suffered from his usual pre-show jitters before each opening night onstage, the final moments before going on the air that first night had him practically trembling in his *Fire Chief* costume. It didn't help matters much when Graham reminded him just moments before air time that twenty million people were going to be listening to him. Although Ed was already a thirty-year veteran of show business, his anxiety now was heightened still further by how his radio listeners across the country might react to his new

venture. "How can a man please twenty million people?" he asked rhetorically. "The answer is he can't. No man is that funny."

Prior to this point, Ed could get over his usual bouts of opening night stage fright within the first few minutes after stepping in front of the audience. Seeing them sitting before him, laughing along with his outrageous puns and antics, always put him at ease. He could instantaneously see and hear the laughter greeting each gag. It propelled him to the next gag, and the next. But how could he gauge the reaction of twenty million unseen and unheard listeners? Most of them had never even seen him perform. What if they just didn't like him?

Graham greeted the studio audience a few minutes before airtime, reminding them that they need not be silent during the show. Just as Ed was ready to collapse from his anxiety, the show was on the air. That first broadcast, as well as all *Fire Chief* programs to follow, opened not with theme music but with the shrill fire siren and sounds of general mayhem as Ed bounded onto the theatre stage on his way to the microphone. The audience applause eased him into his familiar element. He wore a fireman's hat, coat, and assorted accessories for the benefit of the studio audience. As he once explained, "I can't act funny unless I dress funny. I have to look the fool in order to play the fool." His mike fright, however, caused his voice to jump an octave, turning it into a cartoonish, high-pitched shriek. Somehow, though, it seemed to fit perfectly.

Variety raved about the show's premiere broadcast, calling it "a splendidly conceived and executed half hour." The review's praise didn't end there: "Serving to mark a double debut on the air, the program evidenced smart headwork behind the microphone giving both Texaco's new brand of gasoline and Ed Wynn a scintillating start. These 30 minutes are apt to become a model upon which future advertising broadcasts will be based, as everything it went after it probed for full worth."

Each program had the same structure, albeit a loose one. Aided by McNamee, who, despite his pre-broadcast joke that first night, provided Ed with moral support as well as on-air straight lines. Ed joked, chuckled, and traded one-liners throughout each half-hour, landing gentle jabs at the sponsor (previously taboo in broadcasting), and pausing for occasional musical numbers by guests and/or the orchestra. He changed costumes a few more times within the half-hour.

He wrote most of each broadcast himself, with contributions by Eddie Preble and others, digging into both his mental encyclopedia of gags, and his files containing thousands of time-honored jokes. "It would be an impossibility for any comedian to create enough jokes to fill a weekly half-hour single-handedly," Ed said. "I don't create all my own jokes; most fellow comics of the air originate none of their own material."

One segment to become a program staple had Ed answering (fictitious) questions sent in by listeners, as read by Graham. "Dear Fire Chief," he would read, "who was the first person to do a jigsaw puzzle?" After thinking a moment, Ed responds, "The first person to do a jigsaw puzzle…was a Scotsman who tore up a ten-dollar bill by mistake!"

Although he was fortunate to have such a vast collection of proven jokes at his disposal, Ed realized the need to come up with fresh ones as well.

"I have never worked so hard on any job in my life as at this job of broadcasting," he said just one month into the show's run. "I've been up until the wee hours of the morning working up new gags

Performing the show on the air.

for future broadcasts. This business of being funny is no joke. In four programs, I have written dialogue that runs an hour and five minutes. Why, by the time the thirteen engagements are filled I will have written enough material for three [Broadway] shows."

This was the toughest aspect of starring on radio that he and every vaudevillian-turned-radio comedian now had to deal with. Their biggest headaches, of the truly migraine variety, came courtesy of the voracious appetite radio had for new comedy material every week. As vaudevillians, they were accustomed to performing roughly the same proven act to local audiences at each stop on any given circuit, and enjoyed the comfort of knowing they were facing a different audience each time they stepped onto the stage. They could use the same material almost indefinitely as they crisscrossed the country. With the advent of network radio, that all changed. Millions of people across the nation could hear a comedian's best material on a single night—material that may have taken months or years to perfect. And those same millions of listeners certainly didn't want to hear the same material the following week. Consequently, a good number of vaudevillians that hoped to make a successful transition to radio soon found their creative wells running dry. A big-time comedian signing a hefty contract to star in his own weekly program would soon feel his self-satisfaction dissolve into near-panic, born out of a need to create, adapt, borrow, and steal *a lot* of comedy material every few days, and still try to keep it sounding fresh. George Burns recalled, "When we all went into radio I don't think any of us realized how much material we would need. Even with all back issues of *College Humor* and *Whiz Bang*, by the end of the third or fourth week we were out of new material. So we began hiring writers to work for us full-time."

For most comedians, hiring a staff of writers to create new comedy on a weekly basis seemed the logical, as well as necessary, solution to any looming gag shortage. But even *this* was a new concept in the early 1930s. The problem with hiring writers was that the first generation of radio comedy writers weren't really so much *radio* writers as librettists brought from vaudeville and Broadway revues. They were just as new at writing for the airwaves as the comedians were at delivering the material. They had to create a new world consisting solely of voices and sounds that could tap into the listener's imagination and elicit laughter. But at least the chore of creating a new show every week could be shared by a staff of writers, instead of weighing on the shoulders of a single vaudeville graduate creating in solitude. There were still some, like Fred Allen (whose first radio program, *Linit Bath Revue* premiered the same year as *The Fire Chief*), who felt compelled to hammer out each program more or less single-handedly, accepting only peripheral help from assistants. While Ed had Eddie Preble, Allen had the likes of future novelist Herman Wouk.

Now that *The Fire Chief* show was on the air, Ed would have to perform double-duty for the following month, working on the radio show as well as continuing onstage with *The Laugh Parade* at the Imperial Theatre. He was earning $7,500 a week with the show, plus another $5,000 for each *Fire Chief* broadcast.

The Laugh Parade ended its Broadway run on May 21, after which Ed took a summer break, and began preparations for the show's national tour in September.

A little known, and stillborn, side project of Ed's had its beginnings shortly before the tour began in the autumn. While he was never to pen his autobiography, he did begin a book, tentatively titled *The*

Philosophy of a Fool, reportedly a collection of his articles and essays about comedy. Ed apparently had the intention of retaining all publishing rights to the work by creating Keenan Productions, under which the book would be published. Surprisingly, however, he did not want it to see the light of day until after his death. In a newspaper guest column he wrote in 1937, he revealed that the book "is not to be published until I have passed on, and then it will be bequeathed to my son Keenan." Alas, the book was never published, and indeed may have never been completed.

The Laugh Parade began its tour in Boston, on Labor Day. Once there, Ed tried a little experiment to see how influential the radio show had been nationwide in the preceding months. He used his "so-o-o-" tag line, which he was now using fairly regularly on the air, during the Boston performance. "The 'so-o-o' won quite an ovation," the *New York Times* reported, "and Wynn decided that here must be members of the Tuesday night radio audience in the theatre."

The question arose as to how Ed could continue broadcasting the *Fire Chief* show in New York while performing the road production of *The Laugh Parade*. He devised a way that allowed him to come close to being in two places at once. The first part of the tour would be limited to eastern cities such as Providence, Springfield, Baltimore and Washington. Secondly, Tuesday night performances of the stage show would be omitted (with extra Friday matinees added in their place), thus allowing Ed to travel from a city on the tour back to New York each week to do the *Fire Chief* broadcasts. When the tour took *The Laugh Parade* to points too far from New York to allow such a commute, he would broadcast the radio show from whichever theatre *The Laugh Parade* was playing. Thus, Tuesday night audiences that would normally pay to see the stage show were instead treated to a live broadcast of *The Fire Chief*, complete with Graham McNamee and bandleader Don Voorhees along for the ride. And, since the Depression was sinking steadily to its deepest depths at the time, earnings from the charged admissions on the *Fire Chief* broadcast nights were donated to local charities for feeding the unemployed and homeless. Stops along the tour included Chicago, Kansas City, St. Louis, Toronto, and Buffalo, before *The Laugh Parade* finally returned to New York in mid-February, and Ed returned to his broadcast studio atop the New Amsterdam Theatre.

One year into his stint as the Fire Chief, he was already feeling tinges of creative fatigue that would plague so many of his on-air contemporaries. The ratings were good—he would finish third behind Eddie Cantor and Jack Pearl in '32—but radio's merciless appetite for funny material began to wear on him. He couldn't tap into his treasure trove of visual comedy for the show—not to any great degree, other than donning costumes and mugging for the studio audience. Performing for the strictly verbal medium for Ed was like working with one hand tied behind his back. "I've always been accustomed to cavort about the stage at random," he said. "And now I find myself glued to the spot with a script before me. How can anyone be funny facing an audience with a manuscript in his hand?"

Keenan, for one, never thought Ed and radio were a good match. "He was a clown. A great clown," he explained decades later. "He was a visual clown. Now, unfortunately, he became tremendously successful in radio, where he could not be seen. He was not a joke comedian...Now all of a sudden this man was locked into what he had never done. He was visual. He was suddenly locked into coming up with fifty-five jokes every week on the Texaco show."

Fred Allen saw the limitations of Ed's presentation style, and that of similar radio comedians who crammed their broadcasts with as many jokes as they could fit in. "It seemed to me," Allen later wrote, "that the bizarre-garbed, joke-telling funster was ogling extinction. The monotony of his weekly recital of unrelated jokes would soon drive listeners to other diversions." Allen took a different route, choosing a more situational comedy formula, as did Jack Benny. It was purely a matter of which style best suited each comedian.

It was during the 1933 season when Ed began to hear some grumbling among some listeners about how some of his jokes were beginning to sound familiar (he estimated receiving 300,000 letters during his first year on the air). He was a bit perplexed, and a little hurt, by the complaint, and responded in an interview with a bit of grumbling himself, armed as always with a few pointed statistics. He noted that he told an average of fifty-nine jokes per program, totaling about 3,000 gags in a single year of *The Fire Chief* broadcasts.

Furthermore, out of his personal file of more than 200,000 jokes, "approximately 200 possibilities are discarded for every one that is included on a program. Most of them are new; a few may be old. And still a listener will write to say, 'Last week I was surprised to hear you tell two old jokes.' They will not put it this way: 'Last week you told fifty-seven new ones.' And yet that is the average I have maintained each week."

Many of his fellow comedians might have shrugged off charges of repetition, but Ed took his comedy seriously, and took the criticism to heart. What's more, he felt that, as the top stage comedian in the country, and one of the top radio stars, he had a reputation to protect. He knew intellectually that there would be some radio listeners who just wouldn't warm to his style. Emotionally, however, he found that idea difficult to deal with, confessing that "there isn't a Tuesday that I'm not as nervous as a man who faces a death sentence."

Occasional listener complaints notwithstanding, *The Fire Chief* continued humming along (or, more accurately, giggling along) throughout 1933. Ratings were high enough to keep any radio star happy. One survey that season calculated that 74% of Tuesday evening radio listeners were tuning in to the show at its 9:30 time slot.

A story appearing in print at the time reported that two East Hampton, Long Island firemen were having dinner at a local restaurant when the program's signature fire siren emanated from the eatery's radio speaker. The two immediately jumped from their table and rushed out to answer the call, only to return a short while later, visibly embarrassed by their own hasty reaction.

The Fire Chief also became quite the merchandising bonanza for Texaco. Aside from the wave of print advertising for the gasoline, Ed's goofy Fire Chief image inspired a wide range of items, including wall clocks, children's games and toys, story books, dolls, and masks. He had made the transition from Broadway star to national sensation.

By the mid-1930s, radio comedy had hit its stride, as the top comedians in the business filled the airwaves with both variety and situation comedy formats. For that first crop of favorites, their transition from vaudevillians to radio stars was complete, and their

Fire Chief game box cover.

mastery of writing and performing on radio become stronger with each passing year. What originally developed out of necessity had grown into a sophisticated art form.

As Jack Benny explained:

> "In radio's golden age we...Hope and Wynn and Cantor and Fred Allen and Edgar Bergen...we invented a new technique of communicating comedy situations. We learned how to orchestrate voices, sound effects, pauses, silences, and scenes for the *ear*...Now you could pick up one of our scripts and read it and read the sound cues and the dialogue and maybe it would not be very funny. Well let me tell you something. We didn't write to be read the way S.J. Perelman or Robert Benchley or James Thurber wrote...We wrote and acted to be heard. We wrote pictures, made out of various sounds and voices."

Although radio became *the* next step for those who had toiled on the stage for so long, in countless vaudeville and burlesque houses across the country, it never promised to be a sure thing for anyone. Not every accomplished stage comedian keen on a radio career was as lucky as Ed or Eddie Cantor to find a niche on the air. Big names from the stage like Bert Lahr, George Jessel, Groucho Marx, and Milton Berle all found limited success, or even outright failure, in their early attempts to parlay their vaudeville and theatre triumphs into radio popularity. Berle alone would have a half-dozen radio shows within a ten-year period, none of which suited his brash, impatient delivery. Groucho also made several attempts at starring in his own show, determined to conquer the medium as he had Broadway and films, but he had to settle for being a popular guest on numerous variety shows (his own hit quiz show, *You Bet Your Life* would not premiere until 1947).

Despite achieving such a major professional victory on radio, the next few years for Ed would bring a shift in the ratio of victories to defeats, both professional and personal. And the defeats began to come in disturbingly quick succession.

Chapter 7: Disappointment

"Wynn, the undefeated, is protected by the god of war who loves courage, and the god of little children who loves clowns."
—Radio Stars, 1935

In the early spring of 1933, a group of businessmen approached Ed to head a new radio network, to be known as the Amalgamated Broadcasting System, which set up shop at 501 Madison Avenue in New York. One of the network's goals was to relegate sponsor's commercial announcements to the beginning and end of each program, while encouraging listeners to seek more information about the sponsor's products in the next day's newspaper ads. The overall plan was to set up a chain of network stations on the East Coast first. Two weeks after that, it would then expand westward as far as Chicago, eventually forming a system of 100 stations. The sales pitch sounded sweet enough to interest Ed in taking on a new job as network president. Part of the agreement meant taking himself and the *Fire Chief* program from NBC. Of course, Amalgamated wasted no time promoting Ed and *The Fire Chief* program as its first client.

From the start, the plan was poorly organized and executed, causing delays and loss of interest among the potential affiliates. Despite initially lauding the project with great optimism in the press, it wasn't long before Ed found himself feeling a case of buyer's remorse, and seemed to lose interest in his role as network executive almost as soon as he accepted it. He had been spending the past year performing both on stage and on radio virtually simultaneously, and was now serving as the president of a new network. Yet, even with so much on his plate, he managed to overextend himself still further.

The latest opportunity to attract his attention came when MGM made an offer for him to star in what would be his third motion picture feature (and second sound film). Despite the disappointing results of his first two pictures, Ed had reason to feel optimistic about this one. The director this time was to be Charles Reisner, who had worked with Keaton and Chaplin. The talents of Bert Kalmar and Harry Ruby, authors of the brilliant screenplay for the upcoming Marx Brothers' *Duck Soup*, were also called upon. It was announced that Reisner would go to New York to collaborate with the team, while Ed worked on incorporating ideas from both his stage and radio shows into the script. This excited him, as it was his first real opportunity to combine his favorite visual *and* verbal gags in one picture. In his mind it would be the next best thing to doing it all on television. The title of the film was to be, appropriately enough, *The Chief.*

He set out for Hollywood in May of '33, arranging to continue broadcasting the remaining radio shows of the season from there as well.

Career-wise, Ed was riding high. In the past year alone, *The Laugh Parade* kept its audiences happy while making its star the highest paid performer on Broadway. Concurrently, *The Fire Chief* show presented his silly, chuckling character to listeners across the rest of the country, while also making him the highest paid performer on radio. He became a multi-millionaire during the very depths of the Depression. And he enjoyed spending his money lavishly, but he did so not solely on himself and his family. He listed as many as twenty-seven dependents at the time, mostly relatives and friends who knew him to be a soft touch. His "payroll" for them amounted to more than $37,000 a year. When asked why he was so generous with his money, Ed replied, "I have no desire to be the richest man in the cemetery."

And now he was in Hollywood, hoping to achieve the show business trifecta: success on stage, radio, and film.

"I'm stunned by own success," he said at the time. "I don't know what to make of it. I ask myself 'why?' Why me and not my brother, who was born of the same parents, brought up in the same environment? I guess its like the case of the singer who just happens to be born with a song box in his throat—and no credit to him…I believe that the credit for these things belongs to God, or biology, or Nature. The name's unimportant."

Much to his surprise and disappointment, however, the finished version of *The Chief* abruptly dashed his hopes of releasing a quality film that could display his talents to their best advantage. For starters, Arthur Caesar and Robert E. Hopkins are credited with the story, but Kalmar and Ruby's names—and their creative influence—are nowhere to be found. Keenan asserted that no one on the creative end of the film possessed more than a passing familiarity with Ed's comedy.

In addition, the film contained a heavy dose of the kind of pratfall slapstick that did not suit Ed well. While he was indeed a visual comedian, he did not specialize in, nor look totally at ease with, the physical knockabout style of gags that permeates the film.

The story takes place in New York's Bowery in the 1890s. Ed stars as Henry Summers, the son of a deceased fire-fighting hero who becomes a hero himself by somewhat clumsily rescuing a woman from a burning building. Hailed as a hero like his father, he is persuaded to run for alderman, but is unaware that his opponent is a corrupt and sinister incumbent named Clayton. After failing to bully Henry into dropping out of the race, Clayton has Henry's mother kidnapped to get him to quit (the funniest scene in the film shows Ma cooking breakfast and fussing over her captors at their hideout). Henry, panic-stricken over Ma's abduction, decides to act as if he has gone crazy, hoping this would discourage his potential voters from electing him. Of course, Clayton gets his comeuppance in the end, and Ma returns unharmed.

But then the film abruptly and inexplicably switches to a radio studio for a *Fire Chief* broadcast, with Ed, Graham, the orchestra, and audience having a great time. Ed provides a wrap-up of the Henry Summers story theatre-goers had just seen, and then answers a few write-in questions from listeners. The *New York Times*' review called this final add-on scene "a somewhat desperate effort to corral the comedian's radio public." But Ed was spared the brunt of the blame: "It is the finest tribute to Mr. Wynn's comic ingenuity that he persuades his audiences at the Mayfair to laugh at such antique side-ticklers as the release of a water hose into a holiday crowd, the ferocious struggle with a pet bear and the destruction of a valuable vase." The review concluded, "What it all comes down to is that Mr. Wynn is genuinely funny and *The Chief* is not."

After a lukewarm response from the public and the press, MGM decided not to ask Ed back for another film.

It was his third failure in movies, both from a creative and commercial standpoint. His sour experiences naturally produced sour grapes, and turned him into a conspiracy theorist of sorts. He contended that the movie industry, in an effort to kill off radio, coaxed the biggest radio stars at the height of their popularity to Hollywood in order to deliberately put them in bad films. The idea, he believed, was "to get people to go out, not sit home" listening to the radio. Thirty years later, he said, "This has been my contention all these years, and I haven't changed a bit from it." He cited fellow comedians such as Jack Benny, Fred Allen, and Jack Pearl as those who failed in poorly conceived film vehicles.

Ed may have had an interesting contention, but the facts bear him out only partially. It could be argued more convincingly that the popularity of motion pictures caused *vaudeville* to suffer more than radio in the 1930s. Films began to grab more and bigger stars from the bills in America's vaudeville theatres. It has been said that the unofficial end of the vaudeville era came in 1932, when its Mecca, the great Palace Theatre in New York—the last all-vaudeville theatre in America—began including films in its weekly bills along with live entertainment. Other big time vaudeville houses also saw a brighter future by offering movies to their patrons, and began adapting themselves accordingly. It was clear that movies, not stage shows, had become the most popular and financially rewarding form of mass entertainment. Vaudeville, as it had existed for the previous half century, began dying a rather slow death.

The term "Golden Age," in almost any context, is woefully overused. Still, with little doubt, the entire decade of the 1930s proved to be the true Golden Age of American film comedy. This precise ten-year span produced the finest films from the finest comedians in the business. The true comedy titans—Laurel & Hardy, The Marx Brothers, and W. C. Fields—all reached their creative peaks within this brief period, as did Mae West, The Three Stooges, Hal Roach's "Our Gang" (a.k.a. "Little Rascals") series, Charley Chase, Thelma Todd, and others. The sheer volume of brilliantly conceived and performed comedy films at the time, created by the greatest film comedians who ever lived, is staggering. Slapstick reigned supreme, and the most successful slapstick comedians were those who had also created strong comic personalities. Some may say that the 1920s were in fact the Golden Age of Film Comedy. But the silent films by their very nature could not include a verbal element, whereas a sound film could still rely mostly on visual comedy, while doubling its comedic value with its dialogue. Thanks to this, several top radio comedians were able to make their mark during film comedy's Golden Age.

While Ed correctly pointed out that Jack Pearl's Baron Munchausen character starred in a single, unsuccessful film for MGM, other radio pros, such as Burns & Allen, took to films quite well—their stage experience no doubt helped greatly. They signed with Paramount in 1930 to do a series of thirteen shorts, based on their most popular stage routines. The studio gave them prime spots in three versions of *The Big Broadcast* series (1932, '36, and '37). They also starred alongside W.C. Fields in both *International House* ('33) and *Six of a Kind* ('34), appearing in twelve Paramount features in all. In a nutshell, Paramount simply knew how to produce great comedy films, and MGM did not.

Vaudevillian Jack Benny starred in nearly twenty films—his most acclaimed performance being in *To Be Or Not To Be*, a 1942 release (his most famous bomb, *The Horn Blows At Midnight*, came out in 1945, destined to become his own source of self-deprecating jokes). Fred Allen's film debut, *It's In The Bag*, didn't take place until 1945, when Allen had been enjoying his success on radio for over a decade.

So, despite Ed's claim, history shows us that it is unlikely a conspiracy among the movie studios was responsible for the meager results of some radio comedians' forays into film. It should also be noted none of them abandoned radio outright in favor of pursuing motion pictures; they always returned to their microphones. Unfortunately for Ed, after *The Chief*, his movie career, such as it was, would lie dormant for the next twenty years.

Shortly after returning to New York from Hollywood, he took a look at the shambles that was the Amalgamated Broadcasting System (which had its inaugural broadcast on September 25), and officially declared that he wanted out. He began talks with NBC, at which time the network took about twelve seconds to welcome him and *The Fire Chief* back with open arms. He then resigned as president of Amalgamated, citing that he was too busy with other work to keep in touch with the operations of the network, and that he was, to the surprise of no one, a showman and not an executive. Three days later, the whole Amalgamated operation sank for good. The fiasco cost Ed a cool $305,000 out of his own pocket.

The new season on radio in October of 1934 brought with it a new idea Ed wanted to add to *The Fire Chief*. He had never incorporated the "real world" of events in the news into his comedy, but decided to make the change despite his own nervousness about it.

"I'm going to present a humorous slant on big news items," he explained, "something I've never done before. Instead of burlesquing a subject in a humorous vein, I'll burlesque a situation out of the news with a pointed line...And I'm going to try to crowd into fifteen minutes from sixty-one to sixty-five comedy points."

As always, his audience's approval of his comedy was his top priority. This is true of every comedian, of course, but with Ed, it was somehow more personal. "To think that people can still laugh at me after being an actor for over thirty years gives me the greatest pleasure in the world," he said. Having been named an honorary fire chief in dozens of cities across the country, his popularity and the kind words from his fans only reinforced his feeling of responsibility to continue his high comedy standards "to justify all the things they've said to me."

By this time, the program had moved to Radio City's huge new theatre studio. But while Ed thrived whenever he immersed himself in the creative process for the radio show, problems away from the studio continued to mount. Lawsuits and litigation of various kinds dogged him throughout the 1930s, costing him what little peace of mind he might have otherwise enjoyed. One especially painful experience, a family matter played out in public, involved a lawsuit filed in October against Ed by Samuel and Ruth Greenberg, the relatives he arranged to care for Hilda in 1929, during his many extended absences from home in Great Neck. Ruth charged in the lawsuit that Ed had hired her and Samuel as companions for Hilda in order to put an end to her violent outbursts and public harassing of him. Ruth claimed to have "utilized her special art and skill" in caring for Hilda, but still suffered physical injury during at least one of Hilda's private rages. She and Samuel wanted $115,000 for their time, trouble, and out-of-pocket expenses. For his part, Ed claimed that there was never a written, binding agreement between the parties, thus excusing him from financial liability. The litigation dragged into the following year, at one point producing emotionally charged testimony from Ed, who listened to both his own character, and Hilda's, maligned during the proceedings. "Your honor, this has got to stop!" he implored from the witness stand, trembling with emotion. The trial also included reluctant testimony by a saddened, seventeen-year-old Keenan, who denied ever seeing his mother attempt to harm either himself or his father.

Ultimately, the jury ruled that Ed should pay $1,000 to Ruth, although the judge announced after the verdict that he would have ruled in Ed's favor.

When it came to discussing his personal life with the press, Ed seemed to be of two minds. He considered himself a private person, wanting the public to see only his clownish persona, but he would also, on several occasions and without prompting, open up to a newspaper or magazine columnist, allowing for a brief but troubling glimpse into his ongoing melancholy.

"I am the most unhappy man in the world," he admitted to a reporter in the summer of 1935. "Everything that could possibly happen to disturb the tranquility of a man's life happened to me— and is still happening."

He affirmed his belief in the time-honored philosophy among comedians that "in all true comedy, there must be an undercurrent of pathos; and the pathos can only come from the comedian's intimate acquaintanceship with the heartbreaks, the misery, and the elemental sadness of life." And then he would go onstage and send a theatre full of people into fits of laughter.

George Kent's essay in *Radio Stars* magazine that year made an impassioned case for Ed's wellspring of courage in the face of near-debilitating hardships in his life: his blacklisting after the actor's strike, the failure of the Amalgamated Network, and his court case with the Greenberg's. The piece, with its abundance of melodramatic prose, asked, "How long can he go on giving the world contagious *funitis* and *laughobia* when he himself hasn't got them? There's a limit to Pagliacci laughter. How long, I wonder, can a harlequin, with a breaking heart, go on obeying the command: Laugh, clown, laugh!"

On June 4, 1935, *The Fire Chief* aired its final broadcast. Radio was quickly maturing as a medium, so much so that by the mid-decade, Ed's style of comedy was beginning to sound just a touch out of date. With the end of the *Fire Chief* show, he was now without a job, and without his accustomed $7,500 a week salary that went with it. He suddenly had time on his hands, time that he could have devoted to his family, but his relationships with both Hilda and Keenan were already greatly damaged, and ultimately joyless. Without an audience to perform for, Ed simply didn't know what to do with himself. "He was lonely in a special way," Keenan wrote. "He missed an affectionate family life, though it was difficult for him to contribute much to it that we gave him credit for, except money. We didn't always recognize his love. He'd been raised in a fond, strong family, where the mother was terribly important and joys and sorrows were shared. The emptiness he met in his own family from wife and son must have hurt badly."

It's anyone's guess as to who took news of the *Fire Chief* cancellation worse—Ed, or his overwrought advocate at *Radio Stars* magazine, George Kent. Kent's fate is unknown. For Ed, however, the only solution he knew for his emptiness was to look for another audience.

Chapter 8:
The Stage, the Wives and the Troops

> *"There have been times in my life, and at the height of my career, when I wondered whether it was worth the effort. After all, a laugh—what is it? Something that shakes your sides and then passes off. On the other hand a tear—that's something you don't get over so quickly."*
> —Ed Wynn, 1945

Throughout his sixty-five years as an entertainer, Ed had remarkably few professional failures. *Alice Takat* was one of them.

The story of his involvement with this Hungarian stage drama is one of the most unusual of his career. While on vacation in Budapest some years before (probably on the European trip he took with the family back in '27), he saw the play—performed in Hungarian, of course. Ed, despite not understanding a word of dialogue, managed to follow enough of the story to be quite moved by it.

Written by Dezo Szomory, the drama takes on the emotionally charged issue of euthanasia (Alice Takat being a doctor who performs a mercy killing on a friend with an incurable illness).

In 1936, when Ed found an opportunity to buy the American rights to the play, he did so without hesitation, thus becoming the producer of a dramatic work for the first and only time. Jose Ruben adapted the book, while Ed attempted to secure a top star for the title role. His efforts to interest Greta Garbo, and then Jean Harlow, failed to pan out. Austrian actress Mady Christians (who would later star in the stage production of *I Remember Mama*) took the role.

Of the eight hundred hats in Ed's personal collection, his Producer's hat proved to be the poorest fit. Producing a *comedy* extravaganza was one thing, and something at which he had long ago proved to be quite adept. But the world of dark drama was another. And, while Ed expressed tremendous respect for the young and earnest actors in the company, he also found it nearly impossible to relate to them professionally. The actors, likewise, found it equally unnerving to nod and smile through Ed's frequent attempts to lighten the rehearsal process with his unquenchable compulsion to crack a joke whenever the moment seemed in need of one. By his own admission, he was having more fun with the venture than his cast.

"Dramatic actors are all new to me," he wrote shortly before the play's opening night. "I enjoy having them around. They don't pay any more attention to me than they do to a landlady trying to collect the rent. They don't even laugh at my gags...

"They can convince me I am wrong even after I've made up my mind not to give way to their flowery speech...They've taught me many things about the drama that I never knew before." But the real Ed would not be kept down. "Right now I'm producing my first straight play and no matter how serious it becomes I'll have plenty of laughs. As long as they keep such words as motivation and dramaturgy out of my hair I won't complain."

Despite his talent for putting the best face on a discouraging situation, Ed could not snatch success from the jaws of failure, as he had in the early days of *The Laugh Parade*. The show opened on February 10, 1936, to an apathetic reception. *The New York Times* couldn't rustle up much interest. "When Dr. Takat put to death her friend who could not be cured," said the review, "there was the premise that the death would have great effect on those who lived; the argument was not carried out."

Alice Takat closed the following week.

While Ed dabbled in stage drama, some of his comedy contemporaries stuck with what they knew best. Fannie Brice and Bob Hope were the headline stars of the Ziegfeld *Follies*, while Charlie Chaplin's first sound film, *Modern Times*, was playing in theatres.

Ed took *Alice Takat*'s failure in stride, and re-immersed himself in radio comedy. In that ever so brief period between *Alice Takat*'s opening and closing nights, he managed to launch yet another radio show, *Gulliver the Traveler*, on the ABC network.

Based on Jonathan Swift's classic story, *Gulliver* provided both the opportunity and the challenge for Ed to take on a new character, leaving the Fire Chief behind (and not to be resurrected for another ten years). Of course, Ed Wynn would always be Ed Wynn, regardless of whatever character name he adopted for any given radio program or stage production. But *Gulliver* allowed him to place his comedy in more exotic settings. In fact, shortly before the program's premiere broadcast, he claimed, "I've already got more ideas about the role than I know what to do with." The first broadcast aired on Thursday, February 13, before a live studio audience of 1,090.

Despite his high hopes, however, *Gulliver* did not set the airwaves on fire, and ran only until May.

Ed still somehow managed to get not one but two more regularly scheduled programs on the air before the year was out. May 12 saw the premiere of *Ed Wynn's Grab Bag* on NBC, a summer show that ran until August 4. And, by November 4, *The Perfect Fool* was up and running on Saturday nights for the Blue Network. That program was to last for half a year, until May of 1937.

But by now it was obvious that Ed was floundering on radio, unable to recapture the excitement originally generated by *The Fire Chief*. And his competition was stronger than ever. The weekly radio listings of the 1936-'37 season were crowded by those we recognize now as legendary radio comedians. Sunday nights offered Jack Benny. Monday night's highlight was the Burns & Allen show. Al Jolson and Martha Raye were on Tuesdays, and Wednesday evenings included Eddie Cantor's show, as well as Fred Allen's *Town Hall Tonight*.

Perhaps because the law of diminishing returns was catching up to him as a radio comedian, Ed continued to enjoy talking about his eagerness to appear on television. "I'd like to appoint myself a committee of one for eccentric comedy," he said as 1936 drew to a close, "and try to prove to the radio audience that if they think I am funny now, they will like me twice as well in television. I'm not saying this to be vain; I'm speaking purely from a professional viewpoint."

Away from the vicissitudes of life in show business, 1937 was the year in which Ed and Hilda's marriage had become a hopeless case. In his losing struggle to maintain both a marriage and a successful career simultaneously, Ed's career won. He could not bring himself to give show business second billing.

On May 13, he and Hilda divorced in Reno, Nevada. Just over a month later, on June 15, he raised a few eyebrows by marrying Frieda Mierse, a twenty-eight-year-old divorcee. Frieda's major claim to fame to that point was her reign as Miss New York City of 1927. It has been incorrectly printed, more than once, that she was a former Miss America when Ed hired her to perform several bit parts in *The Laugh Parade* back in 1931 (she appeared in five scenes in the show, playing a different character in each). Frieda in fact was only sixteen when she entered the Miss America pageant in 1927. Her only victory then was being awarded the title "most suitable to an evening dress."

The two were married at New York's Marriage License Bureau, with the ceremony conducted by Ed's friend, City Clerk Philip Hines. Another friend, John McKeon, served as witness. After the ceremony, the couple headed to Ed's yacht, the Sea Wynn, moored at a pier on East 26th Street. Perhaps the most ominous aspect of their union was not so much that it became official only a month after Ed's divorce from Hilda, but that he was a good twenty years older than Frieda. Their age difference would prove to play a role in their marital troubles further down the road.

Much to the delight of fans and critics alike, Ed ended 1937 by returning to the Broadway stage, although it was to be a very different kind of experience for him than those of his previous appearances. The show in question was titled *Hooray For What!* and benefited from having some of the best talents on Broadway collaborating on it. The story idea came from E.Y. "Yip" Harburg, who, in two years time, would co-write with Harold Arlen the music for *The Wizard of Oz* (including the signature song "Somewhere Over The Rainbow"). Harburg and Arlen's collaboration for *Hooray For What!* was part of a larger team including the Schuberts as producers. Howard Lindsay and Russell Crouse wrote the book (they would later write the Tony Award-winning book for *The Sound of Music*), and the man responsible for staging the

production was none other than Vincente Minnelli, (although some lists of the credits read "book staged by Howard Lindsay"). Apparently, the division of responsibilities was not as clear-cut as it needed to be.

Rehearsals were disorganized, with no single individual either willing or able to take firm control over the proceedings. Arguments among those on the creative team erupted regularly. Somehow, however, it all came together in time for opening night on December 1, and, in spite of all its problems, *Hooray For What!* was a hit, due in no small part to Ed's established popularity.

What made this stage experience so different for Ed was the fact that he was appearing onstage delivering material written by others. He found it unsettling in the early going, if only because he was so accustomed to having total control of his words and actions before an audience.

"For years I've made up my own lines and spoke them conversationally to the audience," he said at the time. "This show finds me as an actor, instead of a clown. After thirty-five years, I have become just part of the playwright's picture. But there's still some clown in me. You can't kill that!"

Audiences happily found little difference between Ed reciting his own material and that which was written for him.

In the story, he plays a scientist named Chuckles who, in an attempt to concoct a pesticide to rid his garden of fruit flies, invents a gas so terrible that whoever gets hold of it could conquer the world. Sexy foreign spy Stephanie Stephanovich tries to entice Chuckles to give up his secret. In an early scene, with Chuckles standing behind her, she uses the reflection in the mirror of her compact to copy his formula. But creating the formula, as copied from the mirror image, produces laughing gas.

In a later scene, Chuckle's conscience, in the form of a marionette lookalike, nags at him while he tries to sleep. The exchange is very much typical Ed Wynn:

VOICE: You can't escape from me. I am your conscience. I follow you where you go. Even when you sit down to eat I sit down with you.

CHUCKLES: Well, why don't you pick up the check once in a while?

During rehearsals, Ed befriended one of the young actresses in the cast. She was at first relegated to a small part while serving as understudy for star Kay Thompson (who was to play Stephanie), but Thompson was let go during tryouts, and the understudy found herself in the lead of the show. She got to know Ed well, and, sensing his star power kept the other cast members out of his way, decided he could use a friend. If he could also be of help to her with her own budding career, that would be welcomed, too. The young actress's name was Vivian Vance, who would gain national fame more than a decade later as Lucille Ball's sidekick, Ethel Mertz, in *I Love Lucy*.

Predictably, Brooks Atkinson's review could barely contain his excitement over seeing his favorite clown back on the stage:

> "'Hooray for What!' Hooray principally for Ed Wynn. After six desperate years on the radio, the perfect fire-chief fool has returned in a Broadway carnival that opened at the Winter Garden last evening…Yes, Ed Wynn is back, waddling through a whole costume closet of merry-andrew clothes, drooling remarkable imbecilities, and brightening the social season to a shiny polish at last. If you are a disciple of Ed, the stage fool, all you need to know is that he is again telling jokes with more relish and innocence than any one else in the business…and royally entertaining his audience."

Atkinson had company in his praise of Ed's latest efforts. *Stage* magazine reported:

> "Ed Wynn, with all his preposterous costumes and peculiar genius for hilarity still intact, wanders through a lavish musical…The Winter Garden rocks with laughter. The customers mop away tears of joy. How the lovable fool does this, nobody really knows. Partly, of course, with gadgets, secret panels, trained dogs, and the lisp. The authors have given him the finest material he has ever had, including

some comments about the world situation that make sense, in their demented way."

And *Life* magazine succinctly called *Hooray for What!* "the funniest show of the year."

Ed and Vivian regularly got together before their performances onstage. Vance's biographers, Frank Castelluccio and Alvin Walker, write in *The Other Side of Ethel Mertz* that she and Ed once attended a matinee performance of *Our Town* that touched them so deeply, they found it difficult to perform in that night's performance of *Hooray for What!* "After their curtain call," the authors report, "Wynn apologized for their lack of enthusiasm."

Another member of the production, dancer Dorothy Bird, recalled in her memoirs how Ed's onstage antics kept her enthralled day in and day out.

"*Hooray for What!* ran for seven wonderful months," Bird writes. "I received a salary of thirty-five dollars a week and felt that I was the luckiest person in the world. At every performance, I would change costumes quickly so I could stand in the wings and watch Ed Wynn. Although the musicians in the orchestra pit are a rather bored bunch as a rule, they watched him intently, just as I did, to see what new piece of insane business he would bring to each performance."

Hooray for What! ended its run with its 200th performance on May 21, 1938.

It is around this time that some accounts of Ed's life describe him as having had a nervous breakdown of some unspecified nature, brought on by both personal and professional failures. The collapse of the Amalgamated Network, his divorce from Hilda, and troubles with the IRS (resulting in a payment of just over *half a million* dollars in back taxes), have all been cited, both individually and collectively. But this supposed "breakdown" is not given a specific time period, other than some point in the last few years of the 1930s. The term could be considered an exaggeration, considering that Ed was never out of the public eye for long. And, while the years 1939 and 1940 did bring a number of professional and personal setbacks, no trustworthy account has described him as being physically or emotionally incapacitated in any way. Keenan did describe Ed as having had a "nervous breakdown" several years later, in 1946, stemming from hospitalization for a gall bladder illness. But Keenan did not provide any details.

The first of Ed's tribulations during this period came to the fore in the spring of '39. In April, three years after the end of the wrenching trial involving the Greenbergs, he found himself in court once again. And this time the plaintiff was his own wife Frieda, who was suing him for divorce and $250.00 a week alimony. She brought the suit charging "abandonment and inhuman treatment." He denied the allegations, claiming that Frieda had practically begged him to marry her, which he said he did more for her happiness than for his own.

One newspaper account of the legal proceedings focused on a particularly odd piece of evidence presented by Frieda. It was a love letter Ed had written to her a month before their marriage. She offered the letter to the court to counter Ed's claim that Frieda had to persuade him to marry her. As love letters go, this was about as literal and to the point as any a love-struck author has ever composed. Ed wrote the phrase "I love you" seventy-three times, in three columns on a sheet of paper, with the center column written upside down. Frieda claimed that her fifty-two-year-old spouse was a "dual personality," i.e. a devoted and generous husband when people were looking, and a "constant nag" and penny-pincher at home. In his defense, Ed portrayed himself almost as a real-life Henry Higgins from *Pygmalion*, taking Frieda from the chorus and training her in the social graces (he bought her a dictionary before they were married and encouraged her to learn two new words per day). What's more, he pointed out, he even paid the mortgage on her mother's home in Flushing, Queens.

Ed also asserted that during the previous year, Frieda began to drink heavily, and checked herself into a hospital for "a rest cure." But her version of a rest cure was of a very different nature than that of Hilda's hospitalizations. Ed claimed that, for much of Frieda's hospital stay, she spent little time devoted to convalescing, and most of her time going out on the town each night. Indeed, his story was supported when, in July, hospital authorities reported that Frieda was not ill, but that she *was* disturbing the other patients with her late-night comings-and-goings. It got to the point where the hospital staff asked her to check herself out of the facility permanently.

A surprising twist to the marital conflict came in late October, when Frieda withdrew the original divorce suit in favor of a more mutual agreement, albeit one without the possibility of a reconciliation. Their divorce became final on December 12 in Reno, with the details of her cruelty charges not made public.

That same year, Ed was offered a new movie role, but one that he deemed too small a part to accept. Had he taken it, it might have meant a whole new career in films for him. By turning it down, he denied audiences the pleasure of seeing him as the eccentric title character in MGM's *The Wizard of Oz*.

Ed was producer Mervyn LeRoy's first choice to play the Wizard, while LeRoy's assistant Arthur Freed, and E. Y. Harburg, preferred W.C. Fields for the role. LeRoy approached Ed first with the offer, and when Ed turned it down, efforts to secure Fields stalled when the comedian asked for too much money (Fields also claimed he was too busy writing the screenplay for his film *You Can't Cheat An Honest Man*). Of course, the role ultimately went to Frank Morgan, who made his somewhat brief appearance in the film memorable all the same.

Hilda's health continued to deteriorate throughout the summer of 1940. Keenan wrote, "Now she was breaking up physically, so painfully ill with neuritis that even the touch of a hand agonized her." Keenan withheld the news that he and his first wife, Evie, were expecting a baby, to save Hilda the additional heartache of knowing that she would most likely not live to see her first grandchild.

On August 20, Hilda died at Medical Arts Center Hospital in New York at the age of forty-nine. Her death notice in the press was elusive as to the cause of death, offering only that it resulted from "complications brought on by a previous illness."

That autumn, Ed returned to the stage, but this time he was back in charge of the show, both creatively and by virtue of the fact that he invested $100,000 of his own money in the venture. This latest production, *Boys and Girls Together*, was a revue in two acts, with dialogue by Ed and Pat C. Flick. The songs were written by Jack Yellen & Irving Kahal, and Sammy Fain. Ed devised a big opening act to kick off each performance, and rehearsed it for six weeks before the show's premiere with the acrobatic juggling act the Six Willys. As the curtain parted accompanied by the orchestra's fanfare, the group began tossing as many as twenty Indian clubs through the air with great skill. At one point, Ed appeared from the wings carrying a ladder, set it up, climbed up a few steps, and grabbed one of the clubs in mid-air. He stepped down and left the stage with the ladder and club without acknowledging the audience at all.

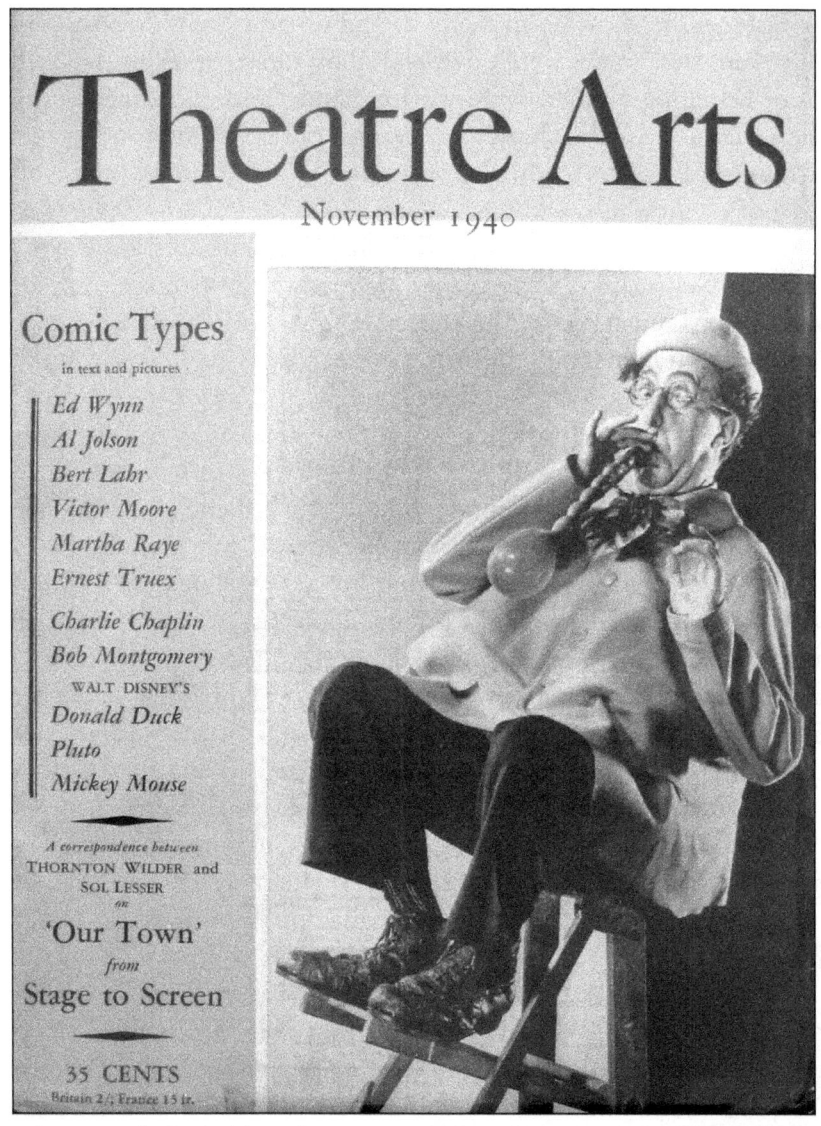

Boys and Girls Together opened October 1 at the Broadhurst theatre.

The review in *Theatre Arts* expressed joy upon Ed's return. "Though his stock in trade is the oldest in the world, though his bag of tricks contains much the same assortment of idiotic oddments as the clowns of all ages have used, in Ed Wynn's hands they become fresh objects of delight and astonishment." However, the review was less enthralled with Ed's job as writer and producer, describing the show as thin, its dating obvious, and its pace slow. But even these faults were downplayed by the conclusion that, with all of Ed's long-winded tales, waving hands, and encouragement of the other acts in the show, "his benign presence gives its daft and irresistible blessing to this latest 'unusual' invention of vaudeville's king of comics."

And, as would be expected, critic Brooks Atkinson was overjoyed not only that Ed was once again on Broadway, but that his comedy was as satisfying as ever: "Just suppose, for example, that Ed Wynn is the funniest man in the world. That seems to be a reasonable assumption on the basis of *Boys and Girls Together*..." Atkinson placed it alongside the earlier successes of *The Laugh Parade* and *Ed Wynn's Carnival*. "It is all very foolish, all very funny. For Ed is a perfect fool out of a demented volume of Mother Goose, and *Boys and Girls Together* is an uproarious one-night's entertainment."

Less than two weeks after posting his review, Atkinson wrote yet *another* column singing Ed's praises. This time, however, he also acknowledged, with considerable sympathy, the fact that his friend's public cheerfulness belied his ongoing private angst. "It is no business of a drama reviewer to comment on an actor's personal calamities," Atkinson wrote, "but this much is legitimate: to endure a series of painful experiences and to emerge unblemished as a superb mountebank without rancor or bitterness is to rear back and pass a miracle." Just for good measure, he also reiterated his view that *Boys and Girls Together* "is funny to the point of tears. It is the peak of Ed's career."

Atkinson was, as usual, by no means alone with his raves. *Life* magazine called the production Ed's "best and barmiest show."

Joseph Wood Krutch, writing in *The Nation*, joined the chorus. "In practice," he declared, "I would not trust either the taste or the character of anyone who did not agree with me that Mr. Wynn's new show, *Boys and Girls Together*, is the best that he ever appeared in and as a delightful an evening of sheer fun as is possible to imagine."

Another critic who attended a performance of the show about two months into its run was someone who did not have a newspaper or magazine column in which to air his views, but who *did* know a thing or two about performing comedy onstage. That critic was

Groucho Marx. In a letter to friend and screenwriter Irving Brecher (author of the Marx Brothers films *At The Circus* and *Go West*), Groucho reported, "Friday night [I saw] the Ed Wynn show. Utterly delightful, a master comic, not a dirty line or joke in the entire two and a half hours."

Boys and Girls Together ended its Broadway run on March 15, after 191 performances, and soon afterwards went on tour.

On the personal front, despite two failed marriages, Ed was not about to give up on the institution just yet. On July 31, he married Dorothy Elizabeth Nesbitt in Las Vegas. Not much was known or written about Dorothy at the time, except that she was the mother of a young boy, John, from a previous marriage.

The year came to a close with the history-altering attack on Pearl Harbor by Japan on December 7, propelling America to war. The entertainment community as a whole responded with a seismic shift in its priorities, and soon motion pictures, Broadway productions, and radio programs were designed not only to entertain, but also to help strengthen the nation's resolve, and to support the newly-drafted G.I.s with songs and laughter. Half a world away from Pearl Harbor, the Nazis' march across Europe throughout the two years prior to the attack was enough to spark the new genre of hyper-patriotic films, as America's entry into the war in Europe became inevitable.

Abbott and Costello became major film stars in 1941, by starring in an astonishing *four* films that year, three of which were set in each of the branches of the armed services. The first, *Buck Privates*, capitalized on the newly instituted draft by having the team (inadvertently) join the army. It was the first, and arguably remains the best and funniest, wartime musical comedy of all. Abbott & Costello quickly followed-up with *In the Navy* and then *Keep 'Em Flying*. All were filmed and released *before* the attack on Pearl Harbor (it is interesting to note that the comedy team's hand and footprints in front of Grauman's Chinese Theatre were set in cement on December 8, the day after the attack).

On March 10, 1942, three months after America entered the war, Ed appeared in a Navy Relief show in Madison Square Garden. The fundraiser for the Navy Relief Society was a mammoth event, filling the Garden's 20,000 seats, a good number of which were taken by servicemen in uniform. The rest seemed to be comprised of just about every American entertainer alive at the time.

In his opening remarks, Fred Allen made a few verbal jabs at show business personalities, plus a few aimed at New York mayor La Guardia. Later in the evening, journalist Walter Winchell reported to the jammed arena that the show had raised $156,000. Boxing champion Joe Louis offered a few heartfelt words (having made an $89,000 contribution to the cause a few weeks earlier).

Martha Raye's message to the Japanese consisted of a hearty Bronx cheer into the microphone, triggering thunderous applause.

As for Ed, he appeared as one of the "Florodora Sextette" along with the likes of Vincent Price, Danny Kaye, and even Boris Karloff, all dressed in drag to varying degrees, for their musical turn.

Other stars appearing that night included Bette Davis, Loretta Young, Jimmy Durante, Jack Haley, Ray Bolger, Merle Oberon, Tallulah Bankhead, Edgar Bergen and Charlie McCarthy, Eddie Cantor, Sophie Tucker, Olsen & Johnson, and many more. The show ran nearly six hours, almost until the dawn's early light.

Later that spring, Ed got busy preparing another new show, *Laugh, Town, Laugh!* in which he would again both direct and host. As he did with *Boys and Girls Together*, he reportedly invested $100,000 of his own money into the extravaganza, and filled the program with singers, trapeze artists, flamenco dancers, and more, all taking their turns onstage as they breathed a bit of life into the aging institution known as vaudeville. There was a fair share of advance hype for the show, since it was to mark Ed's return to vaudeville and his first appearance on Broadway in anything under a $4.40 top price since he took part in the opening of the Palace in 1913.

Ed happily presided as master of ceremonies (one performer with whom he had an unfortunate run-in during rehearsals was a mule named Uno, resulting in a week's delay and a bandage for Ed's hand on opening night). Among the more notable acts he recruited for the show were the comedy team of Smith & Dale, famous for their hilarious "Dr. Kronkite" routine, which was perhaps second only to "Who's On First" as the funniest stage sketch ever. Also on the bill was Senior Wences, the Spanish ventriloquist who was to later achieve national stardom as a frequent guest on Ed Sullivan's TV variety show.

The *New York Times*' opening night review announced, "Mr. Wynn is in high form. With his countless hats, the wondrous costume and the vague, uncertain smile, he wanders on and off the stage, showering puns and inventions."

Time magazine was pleased, if not ecstatic: "*Laugh, Town Laugh* is a likable vaudeville, with Master of Ceremonies Ed Wynn providing the twists, and performers of all nations supplying the turns. Arrayed in his usual unusual costumes and equipped with a few new inventions…the Perfect Fool guides the show insanely from act to act. Wynn is not at his funniest in *Laugh, Town, Laugh*, but he is funny enough; and his embarrassed giggles help to redeem his most embarrassing gags."

Billboard magazine, however, wasn't pleased with Ed's lifelong habit of stealing the spotlight from the acts on the bill as they performed onstage. "He introduces all the turns; he remains onstage whenever possible, attracting as much attention as he can to himself; and he comes on immediately at the close of each act to restart his line of chatter, often when the act's applause is building to its biggest proportions."

Laugh, Town, Laugh was to have the shortest Broadway run of Ed's self-produced shows, closing on July 25 after only sixty-five performances. Discussing the end of the show, he explained that while the evening performances enjoyed healthy attendance, the multiple mid-week matinees suffered badly. He speculated that the cause was due "either to a seasonal slump in afternoon trade or the unfamiliarity of theatre audiences with multiple matinees on days other than Wednesday and Saturday." The show needed to take in $18,000 a week to break even, but failed to reach the mark. It seemed that even vaudeville's master comedian could do little to save the venerable entertainment institution from its ultimate fate.

Laugh Town Laugh was actually part of a wider vaudeville resurgence taking place at the time, especially in the big cities like New York and Los Angeles. It was clear that Broadway itself was no longer a safe haven for vaudeville. The Palace Theatre, which sent shock waves through show business in 1932 by adding motion pictures to its vaudeville bill, began showing double features ten years later. "There are not enough headliners around to insure fifty-two weeks of operation," explained Palace manager Charlie MacDonald.

In deference to changing times, a more polished and streamlined version of vaudeville began to appear in major nightclubs throughout the war years, under the somewhat more sophisticated label "variety revue." Producer/director Paul Small brought favorites Bert Lahr and Joe E. Lewis to *Headliners of 1942*, while another producer, Clifford Fischer, found success with two shows, *Keep 'Em Laughing* and *Priorities*.

Ed's compulsion to work was stronger than ever, even though he, like vaudeville itself, was no longer welcome as a Broadway fixture. So, in March of 1943, he collaborated with Small and producer Fred Finklehoffe and took a new revue called *Big Time* on the road, happily discovering that he could continue doing what he did best, perhaps on a smaller scale than he was accustomed, and still keep audiences laughing just as heartily as before.

Billboard reviewed the show's stop in San Francisco: "Dressed in his weirdest hand-me-downs and most grotesque hats, the puckish comedian is man of all work and acts all over the place. His appearances throughout the show are frequent and funny. In everything he had the audience in stitches with his clowning, utilizing instruments in the orchestra and acrobats for assistance." He closed each performance with his customary exit, holding a candle and wearing a white nightshirt.

In late April, he continued with *Big Time* for a four-week run in Los Angeles, as part of the vaudeville revival in the city. "Two-a-day vaude is blossoming into its former self in this area these days," proclaimed *Billboard*. *Big Time* continued doing good business in other major cities well into the autumn.

With the war effort still a major motivation among those in show business, Ed continued making his contributions to Hollywood's involvement by appearing briefly in the film *Stage Door Canteen*, a star-studded musical extravaganza set in the New York City establishment famous for catering to servicemen and women.

March of 1944 brought with it an opportunity for him to contribute his skills to soldiers recovering from wounds received in the war. He and Gene Kelly set out to travel in two separate revue-type shows organized by Camp Shows Inc., to play the largest army hospitals in the country. Each entertainment unit had its own cast of B-list entertainers, with shows specifically designed to play in hospital auditoriums or ward rooms.

Ed loved the experience, and proudly boasted in later years to have been among the first entertainers to perform for servicemen in military hospitals. He wrote of his visit to the Woodrow Wilson General Hospital in Stanton, Virginia, where he noticed one particular young patient in the ward suffering from severe depression. Ed became determined to summon everything he had ever learned about comedy to make the lonely G.I. laugh. "This boy was all my audiences rolled up into one, all my years in the theatre bunched into a few minutes allotted. If I was ever to justify my existence and career, I would have to help him. 'Wynn,' I said to myself, 'give as you've never given before. Be funny—please!'

Ed reported that he did ultimately succeed in getting belly laughs from the patient.

Chapter 9:
Waiting in the Wings

> *"Ed Wynn started a night club engagement the other day and Broadway was bathed in sentiment, an honest nostalgia for an age that is in temporary decline, the age of the clown."*
> —*The New York Times*, February, 1948

In September of 1944, radio beckoned once again. More accurately, Ed beckoned radio, devising a concept for a new fantasy show, *Happy Island*. He cast himself as King Bubbles, a kindly monarch who takes in refugees from the wicked Worry Park and Isle of Castor, and who oversees their new-found fun on Happy Island. The Borden dairy company sponsored the show, agreed to pay Ed $5,000 a week, and even consented to produce each show on a fully decorated stage, and with the cast in full dress. The most popular of his on-air subordinates were singer/actors Evelyn Knight and Jerry Wayne. Mark Warnow led the orchestra. And, of course, the program offered a heavy dose of Borden mascot Elsie the Cow, and intrusive commercials interwoven into the dialogue.

Ed had been off the air for seven years, claiming that he was waiting for the right time to pursue his idea of total escapist fantasy on radio. "I sincerely believe that we have something refreshing to offer the public," he added.

It is perhaps all the more jolting that even as he was touting the new fantasy land for his radio listeners, he confessed to a reporter that "for over twenty-five years my private life has been hell." The juxtaposition between the childlike frivolity he manufactured for the public and the melancholia he experienced in private, was something he would never easily reconcile.

Happy Island premiered on September 8, on the NBC Blue Network, and most observers were happy to have Ed back on radio. "Seven years away from the air, fortunately have not changed Ed," wrote Jack Gould of *The New York Times*. "His is the love of the idiotic stuff and nonsense that is pure make-believe...On the air was a capital performer rollicking through a tidbit of escapism, and it must have been a dyspeptic listener who could not smile when he was on." The heavy-handed commercials, however, were considerably less welcome: "Every time Mr. Wynn tried to build a little of the illusion of Happy Island for the listener there would be injected, without change of mood, the mundane and too frequent appeal to our buying judgment."

Time magazine shrugged off the program's crass commercialism: "Though his new program is heavy-laden with Elsie the Cow, singers of both sexes and commercials which are part of the plot, Ed Wynn manages, as he has for 42 years of show business, to make the show entirely his own."

But the program had its detractors. Lou Frankel of *Billboard* was apparently one of those dyspeptic listeners. He called the production "amateurish," and said of its laugh value, "it is humor, not comedy; it tickles, not tackles, for howls, with few exceptions." He also did not like the *Happy Island* stage decor, calling it "too decorous," and suggested the program "should be on later in the evening where it might find a more hep studio audience: right now, they sit on their hands, give the cast no help."

The program's history was fraught with problems nearly from the start, even without Frankel's journalistic heckling. The most worrying problem was the disappointing ratings. By early November, three writers had been fired to cut costs, and tinkering with Ed's original concept of the show became a matter of course. In January, Borden announced that not only would the show change time slots (from Fridays to Mondays at 9:00), but it would also have a new name, *The Ed Wynn Show*, reflecting a complete change of format. There would be no more *Happy Island* fantasy, just a straight situation comedy with musical interludes. The announcement added, "Wynn will adopt a Frank Morganish character, who's an expert on everything." (In this ironic twist, Ed was being asked to emulate the same comic actor who, five years earlier, had taken the career-defining role as the Wizard of Oz that Ed had turned down). Evelyn Knight was dropped from the program, but Minerva Pious, popular for years as Mrs. Nussbaum on "Allen's Alley," was added.

In February, Borden finally put the series out of its misery, citing poor ratings and heavy expenses for such things as scenery and costumes. Of course, most programs had always managed to do without visual frills. After all, it was radio. But Ed enjoyed the theatrical ambience surrounding him as he performed in front of the microphone.

In an interview five years after the show's cancellation, he made the curious claim, "I flopped because I had to stick too closely to prepared lines." In more general terms, he had lost the creative independence to which he had grown accustomed, and his opinions mattered little compared to those of the sponsor's accountants and executives.

Through it all, in the twelve year span beginning with the exciting premiere of *The Fire Chief* and the quiet departure of *Happy Island*, Ed continued to keep a watchful eye on television's progress. He was eager to see it evolve from a crude, experimental piece of technology to new and powerful window to the world, finding a home in a choice corner of each American living room.

In 1944, television was still four years from its inaugural full season of regularly scheduled programs. On December 13, Ed addressed 1,000 guests attending the Television Broadcasters Association conference at the Commodore Hotel in New York, giving his speech during the closing luncheon of the conference. He spoke of how his realization of television's potential for greatness made him "get serious for the first time in my forty-three years on the stage and radio."

He called TV a "thing more dangerous than dynamite or the quintessence of good, depending on how it is managed. I should like to advocate a Government-supported television theatre, to which the great body of American actors and actresses might look forward as the climax of their careers, and to which they can adapt their art." It could be argued that, with this remark, Ed described a network entity amazingly similar to what we know today as PBS.

Such lofty goals notwithstanding, World War II continued to delay television's development for public consumption, but its

promise to become an exciting new medium for the masses felt within reach.

In 1944, the NBC network even ran a magazine ad, assuring readers that television will indeed became available not long after the war's end. The ad featured a publicity photo of radio favorites Fibber McGee and Molly (Jim and Marion Jordan), with Fibber almost buried under an avalanche of his famous closet full of junk. The photo was placed within the frame of a TV screen, accompanied with the copy reading:

> "Yes, on NBC Television that crowded closet at Wistful Vista...could all become real visual experiences—experiences for you to watch as well as hear. Already, plans—within the limitations imposed by wartime—have been placed in operation by NBC—plans which with the co-operation of business and government will result in extensive NBC television networks...gradually providing television after the war, to all of the nation."

Interestingly, *Fibber McGee and Molly*, while chosen for the ad's visual message, was one of the *last* radio series to make the transition to TV, premiering in September of 1959 (with a different cast than the radio show). It lasted only half a season.

But the point of the ad was that network TV was just around the corner, for real. In the meantime, radio was still the only viable way of entertaining audiences across the country instantaneously. By this point, however, Ed found himself growing tired of radio's inherent limitations. He had made *Happy Island* as visual a production as possible for the benefit of his studio audience, almost as if he was trying to turn radio into television through sheer will.

On Christmas night of 1945, the Blue Network aired a two-hour program called "Christmas on the Blue," with portions broadcast from both New York and Los Angeles. Ed took part in a sketch with Keenan, who was beginning to establish himself as a solid character actor. Ed, in fact, broke character in his first minute on the broadcast to give his son a sincere and glowing introduction. He wanted everyone to know how genuinely proud he was of Keenan's success, which Keenan had insisted on earning himself, without his father's considerable influence in show business. But the ensuing performance itself was less than a stellar moment for either father or son. After a few more improvised remarks from Ed, a flustered Keenan—with obvious annoyance in his voice—reprimanded his father on the air for not supplying the proper cues as written in the script. It was a brief but awkward moment, and by any measure, not a very professional gesture, exposing the younger Wynn as not being quick enough on his feet to make a smoother segue into the sketch.

In January of 1946, Ed resurrected the *Fire Chief* character for a 4-week period on James Melton's program, but he did so seemingly to kill time, rather than to present any fresh comic ideas to the radio audience.

Two months later, he was briefly hospitalized for a gall bladder illness. Keenan, as mentioned earlier, wrote that the gall bladder attack "had some complications in the shape of a nervous breakdown. He was kept in for two weeks."

In July, Ed finally sold the Kensington house at 19 Arleigh Road in Great Neck. He was now residing in Manhattan on Park Avenue. He was also beginning to notice that requests for his services were becoming fewer and farther between. As beloved as he still was with the public, his last couple of Broadway revues had rather brief runs. He had, by now, all but abandoned radio, except as an occasional guest. There was no chance him starring in his own program again, despite an announcement in the summer of 1947 that he might star in a new series with Keenan. The word came and went without anything materializing. All the while, Ed awaited network television's arrival, much in the way an eager boy visits a construction site each day to watch raw building materials take shape to become a formidable skyscraper. And he wanted to get in on the ground floor.

He still wanted to work in some capacity, so he turned to a venue with which he had no previous experience: the nightclub. He was still a vaudevillian at heart, and would remain so for the rest of his life. So, In January of 1948, he put together an act for Nicky Blair's Carnival nightclub at the Capital Hotel on 51st Street. The show, called "The New Look Revue," included co-stars Jane Pickens (of the Pickens Sisters singing trio), the comedy acrobatic act The Remys (Dick and Dotty Remy were among Ed's favorites), and a bevy of chorus girls. While such a gig might appear as a comedown for such an established and popular star, Ed remained humble to such a degree that he made a gesture virtually unthinkable in the show business universe: he asked the management for a cut in his own pay.

The original deal with the club gave Ed a weekly $7,500 salary for a two-week stay. By the end of the first week, however, he asked for a $2,500 cut, citing his inexperience at a cafe venue, and seeing no reason why the club should suffer for it. He need not have worried. "If any nitery in town can make a buck," *Billboard* noted, "this one should do it. It not only has a show that moves skillfully, but it also has Ed Wynn on top to give it name value."

Ed should have also been reassured by the thunderous ovations he received each night, both upon his initial entrance onstage, and with his familiar closing, in nightshirt and candle, headed for bed. "The applause could literally be heard outside," *Billboard*'s review continued, "Wynn hasn't made any concessions to the nitery formula of today. There wasn't a blue line or even a slight eyebrow raiser in the whole act. It consists of the same gags, the same crazy inventions and the same helpless confusion that made him so great years ago."

Also keeping with his onstage tradition, Ed worked his way into most of the other acts on the bill, with his ad-libs helping rather than detracting. The show was extended several weeks beyond its scheduled engagement.

Upon completing the gig at the Carnival, he moved on to the enormous 6,000-seat Roxy Theatre, with a slightly altered show—this one titled *Scooda Hay* (due to his extended stay at the Carnival, opening night at the Roxy had to be postponed from March 31 to April 14).

For this show, a male quartet kicked things off with a medley of songs associated with Ed, ending with the siren from the *Fire Chief* days. Ed began his remarks by introducing himself to the younger generations in the crowd as "Keenan Wynn's father." Other performers included singer Hollis Shaw, whom the Marx Brothers claimed as their protege with her appearance on their 1938 radio show. She obliged Ed with song as she rode atop his pianocycle. Comic acrobats Dick & Dotty Remy returned as well.

Despite high expectations, the show did not generate a healthy revenue, no doubt due in part to the sheer size of the venue. The first week brought in $65,000, the second week $54,000, and a reduction in the number of daily performances. This time, there would be no extension of the show's run in New York.

April also brought an unexpected offer for Ed. He was asked to return to the Broadway stage—not as a clown in a revue, but as an actor in a legitimate play. The comedy hit *Harvey* was in its fourth year on Broadway when producer Brock Pemberton needed a temporary replacement for star Frank Fay, who was in need of a vacation. Pemberton approached Ed with the offer. But Ed's doubts about his own acting talents quickly put the kibosh on the proposal.

"I just couldn't do it, Brock," was his reply. "If I had to deliver a legitimate line like 'I don't know where Cora is,' I wouldn't know how to. I'm not an actor. I'm a clown." Indeed, with the close of *Laugh Town Laugh* back in '42, Ed never again appeared on the Great White Way in a regular stage show.

On July 1, Ed's older brother Leon died at the age of sixty-five. Unlike his stage struck brother, Leon stayed with the family millinery business in his younger years, while Ed pursued his show business obsession. However, Leon eventually entered the entertainment world as well. After an association with the Schubert theatres in Philadelphia, he became manager of the city's famed Walnut Street Theatre in 1942.

Radio continued to flourish throughout the 1940s, but as the decade drew to a close, radio comedy was beginning to show signs of creative fatigue. Most of the veteran radio comedians at the time were also the very same veteran *vaudeville* comedians who first tackled the airwaves almost twenty years earlier. There were precious few newcomers joining radio's comedy roster who could match the popularity or talents of Jack Benny, Fred Allen, Eddie Cantor, Edgar Bergen, or Bob Hope (the most notable exception being the up and coming Bob & Ray, the last great comedy team on radio). The established stars continued to struggle with the medium's insatiable appetite for new, quality material every week. And the task became increasingly difficult with each passing year, as comedians faced the very real dangers of repeating themselves, growing stale, and ultimately boring their longtime listeners. Some comedians began to experiment with different program formats, hiring and firing longtime supporting players and writers in an attempt to shake things up. In truth, they were damned if they did, and damned if they didn't. Not only that, but once the war was over, television was finally ready to present its first regular prime time season. Some of radio's top stars were feeling tinges of exhaustion, frustration, and in some cases, apprehension. Edgar Bergen expressed his desire for a lighter workload at the time when he grumbled, "I sometimes wonder why comedians like Benny, Bob Hope, Fred Allen and myself should be responsible for full half-hours of entertainment every week. The time has come to give listeners quality instead of quantity. We're all under the gun every Sunday."

Speaking of Bergen, he was actually the first radio comedy star to appear on broadcast television. The ventriloquist, who defied all logic by becoming one of the most popular comedians in radio history (think about it: a ventriloquist on radio), took a stab at television on *Standard Brands' Hour Glass Program* on November 14, 1946. He was, of course, accompanied by his enormously popular wooden partner, Charlie McCarthy, as well as his other companions, Mortimer Snerd and Effie Klinker. Not too surprisingly, Bergen's performance was underwhelming. "It proved once more," reported *Newsweek*, "that television has a long way to go even to catch up with radio's form of entertainment...The only time this crew struck a familiar spark of humor was when Bergen dusted off a vaudeville routine, playing doctor to McCarthy's unrealized tonsillectomy. Otherwise, he floundered vaguely in the unfamiliarity of a television set."

Even performers who were becoming disenchanted with radio were still planning to stick with it, but radio's reign as the dominant home entertainment force was fast coming to a close. And, even though many comedians, like Jack Benny, assumed it would simply continue to exist as it had for the previous twenty years—side-by-side with television—there were others, like Fred Allen, who saw television as nothing less than radio's Grim Reaper. Allen knew in his heart that television, even with its small, fuzzy black and white pictures, was too new, too exciting, and simply too mesmerizing by comparison. By this time, radio's death was all but inevitable. It needed only someone to come along to hammer the final nail in the coffin.

The person with that hammer was Milton Berle. In a dress.

Chapter 10: TV or Not TV

> *"It was murder. It was a rat race...In those early TV days, it was very, very difficult getting new material every week. For the first year I was on, '48 and '49, I didn't even have a writer. I just remembered what I did for the last twenty years, cause we couldn't afford a writer."*
> —Milton Berle

In May of 1948, NBC announced that it was in negotiations with Milton Berle to have him serve as the host of a new variety show, *Texaco Star Theatre*. The idea was to revive vaudeville for television, just as it had thrived at the Palace Theatre for thirty-five years (plans to actually produce the show from the Palace were quashed by union difficulties). It would be the first NBC program to have a studio audience. Another early idea was to use rotating hosts for the show; names on the short list included Al Jolson—and Ed Wynn.

On September 21st, *Texaco Star Theatre*, starring Berle, debuted. Of course, he would remain the sole host of the program, as his presence quickly transformed a fledgling new medium into perhaps the most influential and important facet of American popular culture for the next fifty years. Due in part to Berle, sales of TV sets across the country took off. It has been estimated that TV ownership grew from less than 2 percent of U.S. homes when his show premiered, to over 70 percent by 1956 (when the revamped version of the show left the air). Americans' habits began to change, as they re-arranged dinner dates and social commitments in order to sit in front of the small screen with the fuzzy black and white picture. Some restaurants purchased televisions to lure potential customers, and were sure to mention the new feature in their advertisements, rather than lose business to home-cooked meals (or those revolutionary TV dinners) enjoyed by families watching at home.

Berle alone could not claim sole credit for creating this seismic shift in American pop culture, but he was the catalyst. Before *Texaco Star Theatre* premiered, many consumers needed a reason to actually go out and buy their own television sets. Conversely, television needed a program and/or personality capable of making a strong enough impact to demonstrate that TV was here to stay as a major entertainment force. Berle supplied both the program and the personality. Beginning with his success, TV launched countless legendary careers, saved others, and even hastened the demise of a few. For some performers, it did all three. It also further fueled the success of well-established comedians who had already achieved their fame elsewhere.

Berle had been working as a vaudeville emcee and comedian since he was 16. But he had trouble duplicating his stage success on radio, where he starred in no fewer than ten failed programs, but proved to be perfect for television (he actually first appeared on an experimental transmission in Chicago in 1929). His program was, as intended, a televised vaudeville show, giving him ample room to engage in kind of silly, over-the-top slapstick and time-worn jokes for which audiences loved him. He would often burst onstage dressed in drag or in ridiculous costumes of all kinds, interrupting other acts, true to his anything-for-a-laugh philosophy. Behind the scenes, however, he was a notorious perfectionist and supervised seemingly endless rehearsals with a stern hand. Stories spread of how insufferable he was backstage in the days and hours before airtime each week. But both the program, and Berle himself, would win Emmys for the 1949 season.

With the 1948-49 season the first to offer a full schedule of network programming, the comedy floodgates on television were open. Other variety shows and revues would soon populate the tube, and some observers at the time referred to TV as "vaudeo," i.e. traditional vaudeville peppered with the program sponsors' heavy-handed commercials. For most of the next decade, vaudeville, the remnants of which survived only in the form of nightclub variety revues, found itself resurrected virtually intact, this time for the benefit of television cameras. The comedians, singers, dancers, plate spinners, and jugglers were in demand once again, not only on Berle's program, but also on Ted Mack's *Original Amateur Hour* and, of course, Ed Sullivan's *Toast of the Town*. (later renamed *The Ed Sullivan Show*). At this phase of television's young life, however, it would be the comedy stars, and not the aspiring plate spinners, who would benefit the most.

The comedians who first ventured before the cameras to host their own programs, under sweltering studio lights, did so with a number of uncertainties. While television at first appeared to be some sort of odd blend of theatre, film, and radio, it was in fact none of these.

So, what *was* television, then? What would ultimately fill the screen on a regular basis? For the top comedians of the day, it presented an opportunity to expand and enhance their time-honored acts. But for those first few years of network programming, most played it safe, and true innovation was at a premium.

On the plus side, comedians with a more visual bent seemed to have a promising new outlet for their sight gags, whereas those whose careers flourished primarily on radio had to find something for TV audiences to see as well as hear. "With television," wrote Lewis Nichols of *The New York Times*, "no one will particularly wish to see an average-appearing young man reading jokes from a piece of paper. He will want the baggy trousers, the expression, the glasses which are used for effect and not only to see by."

Ed and Dorothy moved to Beverly Hills in June of 1948, basically so Dorothy could enjoy the climate, and Ed could be in closer proximity to Keenan. In the autumn, while Berle was making television history on NBC, Ed traveled the West Coast with a new revue, called *Laugh Carnival* (he title no doubt was designed to invoke the magic of his earlier stage successes). Produced by Paul Small, who collaborated with Ed five years earlier in *The Big Time* revue, this show maintained a high energy level and a strong cast of performers. *Billboard* raved, "Here's a riot of zany fun and a worthy successor to other Paul Small revues...one of the most hilarious two-a-day shows seen here in a long time."

Although Ed had been looking forward to taking his career to TV even before the medium existed in any practical sense, he also knew that his first television venture had to be the right one. He reportedly turned down a dozen offers before the Speidel watch company and CBS asked him to star in weekly variety show. Upon agreeing to the proposal, he insisted it be produced in Hollywood, necessitating CBS to spend $75,000 on new equipment for its L.A. studio. In 1949, he had been a major comedy star for the previous forty years, and was, at one time, the highest paid entertainer on the stage *and* radio simultaneously. His clout was still considerable.

And now, finally, he was witnessing television become a viable medium, one in which he could get in on the ground floor and project both his voice and his image to the masses, a full year before Jack Benny, Groucho Marx, and Burns & Allen would premiere their programs. "Final touches on the show will be made with meticulous care," reported *Billboard* in the weeks before the program's debut, "as Hollywood's video product may stand or fall on Eastern acceptance of its first major offerings." At least there was no pressure.

"This thing [television] is a marriage with the public that will never be annulled," Ed declared. And that's not all he would have to say in the days leading up to his television debut.

He was eager to challenge the mighty Milton Berle for the title of television's top comedian. Not only did Ed promise to "bust TV wide open" with his arrival, but in the excitement of finally realizing his long-standing dream, he let loose a few uncharacteristically brash remarks aimed at Berle. He said of Uncle Miltie, "I've yet to see something original from that man…He'll be the D.W. Griffith of TV—nobody will give him a job in a couple of years." It was an odd comment, not only due to its provocative, even insulting nature, but because Ed himself had long endured criticisms along the lines that much of his own favorite gags weren't exactly fresh. But CBS vice president Harry Ackerman fed the hype by promising the show would be "something entirely new and different" from programs like Berle's and Ed Sullivan's.

Ed assembled a small team of writers to help him grind out material on a weekly basis. An agent arranged for young Seaman Jacobs, fresh out of the army, to meet Ed for a possible writing job on the new TV show. "And when I got to his home, an apartment on Park Avenue," Jacobs recalled in an interview for the Television

Academy video archives, "I introduced myself and he says, 'You can't be a writer, you're wearing a necktie!'"

Jacobs then met fellow writer Jack Ellison. "We worked in [Ed's] apartment," Jacobs said. "We'd bring in jokes, and put them together. But for new material, it was difficult to sell him. He was used to the way he got his old jokes, probably looking through old *Whiz Bang* magazines and things like that. He did have writers, of course, but he'd do the operas. He'd take an opera and use some characters and make a comedy routine out of it."

As was the case with Berle's show, *The Ed Wynn Show* was basically a televised vaudeville show, complete with a famously hammy emcee. As host, Ed continued his personal tradition of offering jokes that were as hokey as ever, although most groan-inducing quips were saved by his clever asides and ad-libs.

The first broadcast aired live on Wednesday, September 22 (the kinescope wasn't broadcast on the east coast until October 6). The first guests included singer/actress Gertrude Nielsen and the dance team The Szonys—not exactly A-list talents, but the bigger names were soon to follow. *Time* magazine wasn't particularly impressed with the premiere. "Wynn, working as usual with all the acts and covered with his zany make-up, had provided little more than a series of ancient-vintage gags." But *The New York Times*' television critic Jack Gould enthusiastically declared, "The monopoly of Milton Berle in television appears to be at an end...With all the aplomb and assurance of the veteran trouper [Wynn] capers before the cameras with ridiculous ease and obviously has opened a new chapter in his long career in the show business. He is all over the stage, yet to astonishing degree preserves that element of intimacy which is so vital to video."

Life magazine saw the program as a likely inspiration for Ed's contemporaries to embrace television: "If Wynn's shenanigans prove as fascinating to a whole new generation as they did to an older one, other Hollywood big names may well be tempted to take the plunge, too."

"As I remember," Seaman Jacobs said of Ed, "he did a stand-up monologue, and use the visual props—visual puns, really...you'd see a hat go across the stage on wheels. 'You've heard of that—that's a roller derby!' Pretty bad puns. But writing for him was a pleasure.

No pressure other than to get it done in time, once he accepted what we gave him."

Hal Kanter agreed that having Ed for a boss was as educational as it was enjoyable. "He was a very funny man," Kanter said, "and I learned an awful lot about comedy from him. He was really a man who understood comedy, and who understood show business—he understood theatre. He was a great man."

Ed's own long-standing star power attracted the top actors, singers, comedians in show business to his program, including Carmen Miranda, Victor Moore, Peggy Lee, Kay Starr, Eddie "Rochester" Anderson, Eve Arden, Virginia O'Brien, Buddy Ebsen, Dick Haymes, Gloria DeHaven, Caesar Romero, Charles Laughton, and Gloria Swansen. Many of his guests who were appearing on TV for the first time, including young singers Mel Torme and Dinah Shore (Ed invited Shore atop his pianocycle to sing a few songs as he pedaled the oversized tricycle around the stage. She was happy to oblige).

And then there were Ed's fellow comedians who made guest appearances. Among the veterans were Ben Blue, The Three Stooges, Joe E. Brown, and Leon Errol. Buster Keaton made perhaps the most memorable appearance, when he joined Ed on the December 8 telecast. In a silent sketch, the two recreated Keaton's first film role (from *The Butcher Boy*, starring his mentor, Roscoe Arbuckle). Taking place in a grocery store, they frequently produced large cards with bits of dialogue written on them, in place of the titles used in silent films.

One of Ed's initial challenges as a television performer was to find the proper pacing for each show. In his stage shows, he was free to improvise and expand his visual bits of business as he told his involved stories and jokes. Any given performance might run longer than the norm, if the comedy spirit so moved him that night. On radio, he learned the importance of sticking to the script to keep a broadcast within the confines of its allotted half-hour. But in the early days of his TV show, Ed and his writers had to find a balance between imposing limits on his habit to walk about the stage and improvise pantomime, and yet avoid rushing through material to get the show done on time. "I'm still figuring out how much I can talk, how much time I can be permitted to walk around the stage, without slowing up the show," he said. "So if we decide in advance that I can spend, say, five seconds in a particular bit of business and no more, we'll finish up under the wire."

It was around this time that a story began to make the rounds about Ed and one of his detractors in the press, Jack Hellman. The story goes that Hellman had written fairly scathing pieces about Ed's TV show when one day he visited the set with the show's publicity man, Henry Rogers. Hellman was known for being a notoriously unattractive man. As he came down the center aisle with Rogers, Ed, who had never met Hellman, spotted him from the stage. "Who's that with Henry?" he asked aloud. "Jack Hellman," came the response. Ed gave Hellman a lingering look. "I'm glad," he replied.

Of the many "firsts" for which Ed has been credited, one in particular has become perhaps the most indispensable for each and every television host who has followed him standing in front of a television camera, right up to today's crop of late-night talk show hosts. And, while his famously silly inventions were never meant to be taken seriously, this one has been taken *quite* seriously for the past sixty years, becoming a staple of TV, for better or worse.

Ed invented the cue card.

To put it more accurately, Ed co-invented the cue card with production assistant Barney McNulty. McNulty began his career at CBS as a studio usher, and took on various odd jobs and thankless tasks around the studio that gave him an unmatched inside knowledge of its workings. Over time, he became an indispensable go-to guy for solving problems, big and small, that threatened the smooth running of various productions.

"Wynn had the concept of a cue system," McNulty explained, "And what he needed was the order of his jokes. So he needed you to have a card which would have a one-word description of what each joke was. So he'd see 'penguin', he'd see 'Broadway', he'd see 'flying boat,' and he would know that's the next joke he was gonna tell. Because he would put himself completely into telling the joke, and when it was over and got a laugh, now he had to know what the next point was. So on Broadway, he did this. He had somebody in the orchestra pit do it for him, so that he always had control of his Broadway shows that way." Ed wanted to have that same aid for himself on the TV show, and asked McNulty to help out.

There was one night in particular, not far into the first season, when the cards became even more important than usual in keeping the show running smoothly. Ed was under the weather the day of the broadcast, and the medication he took was making his mind a tad cloudy. He found McNulty. "He came to me and said, 'Barney, I'm sick, I'm full of pills, I can't remember anything. Is it possible to put the whole show on cards?' Well, I started thinking. So I said, 'Yeah, I'll do it.' So it took me until 3:30 or so, and I printed it, and got the whole show down. I printed everything. You know what? It worked. Because I was trained as a radio operator, I could write 90 characters a minute unendingly, and it was legible, so I could print pretty fast. I could grind the wordage out, and I didn't have any qualms about doing the cards." McNulty positioned himself in the orchestra pit with the stack of cards and helped Ed get through the show. It soon became the weekly routine. And it wasn't long before other TV hosts were requesting McNulty's services.

One time, however, Ed's writers came to McNulty at the last minute with a substantial amount of new material. Unable to write up new cards in time, he placed blank cards among the pre-written cards to indicate to Ed where the new material was supposed to fit into the show. All agreed it would work, except that they forgot to tell Ed of the idea. "So Ed comes barreling off to the wings in the middle of the show. And he says to Hal Kantor, 'Hal, is Barney drunk? Everywhere I look—blank cards!'"

"Ed Wynn was such a great experience," McNulty said. "The man was such a rich human being. Fabulous. Very sensitive, very passionate, very concerned about people, terrific. I couldn't have had a better introduction to television."

Among the Who's Who of guests Ed had on the show throughout its 39 episodes were a young married and very talented couple who, little did they know at the time, were only a year away from changing the TV sitcom form forever. Lucille Ball and Desi Arnaz appeared on the show on Christmas Eve, although they each performed separately with Ed.

When *I Love Lucy* was still in the planning stages, Ball reportedly insisted on having the show filmed instead of being recorded on kinescope because she never had the chance to see herself and Desi on Ed's show. She also assumed those kinescopes had been

Ed with guest Leon Errol, one of his close friends since their days in the Ziegfeld *Follies* of 1914–15.
PHOTO COURTESY OF TRACY WYNN.

Sketch with British actors Elsa Lanchester and Reginald Gardiner.
PHOTO COURTESY OF TRACY WYNN.

destroyed shortly afterward, and wanted her own program to be better preserved for her children and grandchildren's future enjoyment. However, a story in *Billboard* magazine on May 12, 1951 contradicts this, reporting that it was the Philip Morris company, *I Love Lucy*'s sponsor, that decided to have the show filmed in Los Angeles rather than kinescoped in New York. The reasons given included both the low marks given to the kinescope quality of Alan Young's show on CBS, as well as Ball's motion picture commitments in L.A.

Unbeknownst to Lucy at the time, the kinescopes of Ed's show were saved, including the episode with her and Desi. Better still, today many episodes are available on DVD.

Ed's efforts on his show were duly rewarded. The 2nd annual Emmy Awards, presented on January 27, 1950, handed out statues to *The Ed Wynn Show* for Best Live Show, and to Ed himself for Most Outstanding Live Personality. *Texaco Star Theatre* won the Emmy for Best Kinescope Show, and Berle for Most Outstanding Kinescope Personality. In addition, Ed won a Peabody Award that year.

By mid-March, however, problems with the show began to arise. Speidel's sponsorship expired at the end of December, as originally planned. Camel cigarettes then took over. Camel's first move was to shift the show from its Wednesday night time slot to Saturday night. But there it ran up against NBC's popular *Saturday Night Revue*, putting a significant dent into Ed's ratings. Next came talk of budget cuts for the show, and even a possible way to let Camel out of its sponsorship early. The show moved time slots yet again, to Tuesdays at 9:00, but only for the fourteen cities in which it was up against *Revue*. In those Dark Ages of television, program kinescopes were physically shipped to each network affiliate, making it possible for some stations to create their own broadcast schedules without adhering to a uniform network schedule.

Now with the show in its third time slot since September, there was yet another problem to deal with. It was reported that several CBS affiliates in the Midwest had been receiving viewer complaints about the poor quality of the program's kinescopes. CBS sent engineers to L.A. to work on the problem, while considering the idea of moving Ed and his production to New York, where TV facilities were more advanced (relatively speaking) than those in Hollywood. Even though

The Three Stooges rehearse their memorable appearance on an episode first broadcast March 11, 1950.
PHOTO COURTESY OF TRACY WYNN.

Ed's wife Dorothy sits in on a rehearsal.
PHOTO COURTESY OF TRACY WYNN.

much was riding on the success of Hollywood's fledgling kinescope operations, the top CBS brass began shopping around for an available film studio to convert for their purposes, which would enable the transition from kinescopes to cleaner-looking film—not just for Ed's show, but for every CBS program.

In his autobiography, Buster Keaton tells the story of a spontaneous appearance he made on the show, at Ed's request. Keaton had found a funny hat and thought Ed might want to add it to his vast collection. Upon arriving at the TV studio to present it to him, he found Ed in a quandary about a sketch scheduled for that night's broadcast. Ed was to demonstrate custard pie throwing with four of the original Keystone Kops, but he couldn't come up with a satisfying finish for the sketch. He asked Keaton to hurry home, grab his stage costume, and return to the studio as quickly as possible—while also thinking of a finish for the segment.

Keaton did just that. Without any time for rehearsal, even if only for the benefit of the director and cameramen, Keaton joined Ed onstage and explained that if the show intended to include pie-throwing slapstick, Ed needed to know the proper techniques of throwing a pie. Keaton then brought out each Keystone Kop, one at a time, to stand by the bed and receive a hurled pie right in the face. "They had been looking forward to throwing the custard pies and did not like my taking over the job," he wrote. "They had to be sweet-talked into accepting the change I had dreamed up." Keaton threw each pie with a slight variation of technique, building laughs as he did so.

After the show, Ed took his friend aside and told him, "You saved the show for me tonight."

But Camel decided that the ratings for the program failed to justify the cost, and CBS pulled the plug on *The Ed Wynn Show*. The broadcast featuring Keaton and the Keystone Kops would be the last, airing on June 15 on the west coast, and on July 4 in the east. It was an early death for a program that had promised—and in many cases delivered—so much.

In an interview a decade later, Ed expressed his continued fondness for the series, but, with the benefit of hindsight, acknowledged that the style of comedy had become outdated. "I think [the episodes] are excellent. But I think also, if you showed them to new people, the new generation, they would only laugh at the physical stuff in that. Otherwise, I think it would be corny."

He wasn't one to wallow in his disappointment over losing the show. In fact, there was literally no *time* to wallow. Only two weeks after *The Ed Wynn Show* left the air, he made a deal with NBC to star in an upcoming hour-long variety series beginning that autumn, in which he would rotate with three other hosts each month.

So, barely skipping a beat from the demise of his self-titled show, Ed had a new home on NBC for the 1950-51 season, as one of four rotating hosts of *Four-Star Revue*, broadcasting on Wednesday nights. Danny Thomas, Jack Carson, and Jimmy Durante were the other hosts, and this arrangement allowed each of them a few weeks to rest and work on material between hosting duties. But since the show was to be broadcast from a new facility in Rockefeller Center, it would require Ed to return to New York once a month from Beverly Hills.

Television was undoubtedly the place to be for the 1950-51 season, which brought with it the first major wave of stage and radio comedians to the small screen. Just a month before the premiere of *Four-Star Revue*, NBC launched yet another variety show with rotating hosts, *The Colgate Comedy Hour*, airing on Sunday nights. The network corralled Eddie Cantor, Martin & Lewis, Bobby Clark, and Fred Allen to serve as hosts.

With such an impressive roster of major names prepared to take to the airwaves for the new television season, NBC leased the 3,200 seat Center Theatre in Rockefeller Center from RKO, and spent $300,000 converting it into a mammoth television studio. The theatre, boasting an ornate, Art Deco interior much like that of the 6,000-seat Radio City Music Hall across the street, was part of the original Rockefeller Center complex. It had been a stage show and movie theatre venue since 1932. Beginning in 1940, it even presented ice shows starring Sonia Henie on its huge stage, measuring 110 feet wide and 60 feet deep. The new refurbishment for NBC allowed the space to accommodate TV cameras and equipment.

But this immediately posed a problem: Most of NBC's newly acquired comedy stars (except for Ed) flatly refused to perform at the venue. Cantor, Allen, Berle, and Martin & Lewis all considered the theatre and its stage far too expansive for them. Centre Theatre was just over half the size of Radio City, and twice as big as the landmark Palace Theatre, where most comedy veterans reached the pinnacle of their vaudeville careers. From their perspective as stage performers, they feared that many of their more subtle gestures and facial expressions, which would work fine for television, wouldn't project to the far reaches of the cavernous auditorium. It appeared impossible to reconcile the necessity to perform for both the distant upper balcony and, at the same time, for the TV cameras and intimacy of the small screen in America's living rooms. Three of the four *Revue* hosts insisted on broadcasting from a smaller studio in midtown Manhattan.

But the problem was solved fairly easily in January of 1951, when NBC installed monitors in the theatre for the benefit of those in the "cheap seats," who might have otherwise missed the performers' more nuanced gestures. Once that was settled, the other *Revue* hosts joined Ed there for the remainder of the season.

Ed hosted the *Four-Star Revue* premiere broadcast on Oct. 4, with French cabaret legend Edith Piaf as his headline guest. For one segment, he invited Piaf to sing her signature song "La Vie en Rose" atop his "pianocycle." And, while she—like Dinah Shore and others before her—agreed to incorporate the comedic slant into her musical

number, not all observers enjoyed the spectacle. *Variety* didn't have a problem with it, saying that Ed's contraption "detracted not in the least from Miss Piaf's artistry." However, *The New York Times* was positively livid at the sight of such a demure and beloved songbird as Piaf taking part is such an undignified exercise. "Edith Piaf...was the victim last night of an excusable bit of vaudeville trickery," the rant began. "Both Mr. Wynn and NBC lost all sense of proportion. Miss Piaf was forced to sit atop a small piano, which Mr. Wynn had rigged up on a trick bicycle carriage. While Mr. Wynn pedaled the piano around the stage, thoroughly and completely distracting the viewer, Miss Piaf was expected to sing 'La Vie En Rose.' The whole idea was preposterous." The review concluded with a side comment that validated the trepidation of the other NBC hosts at the time: "Both Mr. Wynn and his show were pretty much lost in the gargantuan Center Theatre. Mr. Wynn needs to work in more intimate surroundings."

Ed's subsequent turns as host were well received. Just two weeks after his kickoff broadcast, he was called as a last-minute fill-in for Jimmy Durante. *Variety* described Ed as "a masterful showman...Casual and intimate...broadly whimsical and pointedly witty as his brand of comedy demands, Wynn's solo performance maintained the sock level attained in his initial stint for this show two weeks ago."

The sudden surge of so many of America's favorite comedians joining NBC was the network's successful response to the popularity of Ed Sullivan and Arthur Godfrey on CBS. And this prompted *Life* magazine to run a photo story of their arrival on television in its October 23 issue. Ed received the honor of appearing on the cover. The brief story assessed, in rather lukewarm terms, how the veteran stage and radio clowns had been faring on television to that point: "So far results have not been spectacular," the piece reported. "Some comics, like [Bobby] Clark, have dipped too often into old gag bags; some, like Fred Allen, were uneasy with the new medium." But the piece did end on an optimistic note, welcoming the comedians to their new home on television, and hopeful for them to hit their stride. However, a sidebar story on Allen further lamented his disappointing premiere. The column criticized his obvious unease, as well as his remarks of disdain for television. He was essentially biting the hand that was now feeding him.

Still, many other comedy veterans initially couldn't figure out exactly what to make of television. How, they wondered, does one perform quality comedy in front of the TV camera? The long-familiar requirements suddenly no longer applied. Some of the old rules needed to be discarded, while some new rules needed to be followed to ensure any chance of success. George Burns, for one, discovered

how television "wasn't like vaudeville—in vaudeville if you made a mistake only a few hundred people saw you and you could correct it during the next show; in television millions of people were watching and you only got one chance. It wasn't like radio—the audience could see you; so Fanny [Brice] couldn't play a six-year-old, and Amos 'n' Andy had to be black. And it wasn't like the movies—everything had to be done live. There were no second takes."

Six months after *Life* examined the new influx of comedians on television, the April 10, 1951 issue of *Look* magazine (*Life*'s chief competitor at the time), featured eleven comedy veterans who began a new life on TV that season. The magazine astutely noted that the average age of the group was fifty-five (Ed being the oldest at sixty-four). Clearly, the powers that be felt more comfortable bringing the well-established comedians to TV than investing too much in the younger generation: "The old-timers had audience acceptance in advance," the piece noted. "Critics wrote endlessly about whether they could 'make the transition' to the 'new medium', but *people* just wanted to see them on television. If the old favorites were nervous over TV, they needn't have been: True show values have changed little since the days of the wandering minstrel."

Here's a breakdown of how several of Ed's contemporaries fared in their new TV careers.

Burns & Allen's switch from radio to television in that momentous October of 1950 proved to be a great success, with *The George Burns and Gracie Allen Show* originally airing live from New York every other week for the first two seasons. But Gracie struggled with the difficulties of memorizing a half-hour script. "All I could think about was 'What's the next line?'" she said. "I haven't memorized anything for twenty years…There may come a time when I forget and I shudder at what I'll do then." At the beginning of the 1952 season, it became a weekly series filmed in Los Angeles. Filming scenes out of sequence didn't help Gracie's memorization struggles, but the program added an extra dimension to the still-new TV sitcom format. In each episode, Burns broke through the "fourth wall" to speak directly to the camera, commenting on the plot developments and hinting at what might come next. He also regularly retreated to his work den, where he spied on the activities of his wife and neighbors by watching them on his television!

Jack Benny also first ventured onto TV in October of 1950, for a series of specials. He brought with him the supporting characters—and the actors who played them from his radio show—for the new venture. Benny was one of those longtime radio residents who kept one foot in radio even as he became increasingly comfortable on television—just in case. He maintained his radio show until 1954, while the TV version aired with increasing frequency, until it finally become a weekly series in 1955. Television enabled Benny to visually enhance his persona as a cheap, vain, self-deluded ladies' man. Making the move with him were announcer Don Wilson, Eddie "Rochester" Anderson, Mel Blanc, singer Dennis Day, and Benny's wife Mary Livingston.

Groucho Marx brought his hit quiz show *You Bet Your Life* to television in October of 1950 as well, after three successful years on radio (it was also the first NBC series to be recorded on film in Hollywood). Ironically, due to the highly verbal nature of the show, there wasn't much television could do to make it a more visually interesting program. The format required Groucho simply to sit at a lectern facing a pair of contestants. But at least viewers could see his telling facial expressions throughout his chats, as well as witness an occasional demonstration of dubious talent by a contestant. Groucho's good friend Fred Allen wrote to congratulate him for bringing a refreshing alternative to television's plethora of variety programs. "You are fortunate, I think," wrote Allen, "that your show lends itself so well to the alleged new medium...it is a pleasure to be able to enjoy some good dialogue without having to watch a lot of broken down small-time acts, burlesque bits and tired blackouts. All of the [comedy] shows here...seem to be using the same devices. This should make your half hour a novelty doubly welcome as the season goes along."

Unfortunately, not every radio comedian deserving of continued success was able to find it on the tube, as Allen himself would soon discover.

Allen enjoyed years of tremendous success on radio, and his playful way with the English language brought him the glowing admiration of his peers. His show premiered in 1932, the same year as Ed's *Fire Chief* program, but Allen stayed on radio almost continuously for the next seventeen years, before the ratings declined significantly by 1949. He then felt little choice but to explore the possibilities of television, and famously joked about television being "a medium that's rarely well done." He somehow anticipated that it would create big problems for his career. His fear of TV was genuine, if somewhat difficult to understand. To Allen, witnessing television's arrival was akin to seeing the darkest of storm clouds advance menacingly on the horizon, without any protective shelter within reach. While *The Colgate Comedy Hour* format was certainly well suited for the hosts who often ran amuck with their broadly played slapstick (Cantor, Martin & Lewis, and Abbott & Costello, who joined the show the following season), Allen was the odd man out in this setting. He still had loftier aspirations as a comic voice, but as he witnessed the imminent death of radio and the frenetic pace of comedy on television variety shows, he found no suitable outlet for that voice.

In a letter to Groucho shortly after the *Colgate Comedy Hour* premiered, he lamented, "The revue type of show is the wrong approach. We have to work in a theater with an audience. The cameras can go noplace [sic] and the intimacy is totally lacking. I hope, after a few shows, to shed the audience and attempt to do something with more scope." Allen was dropped from the *Comedy Hour* rotation two months later.

Likewise, Bobby Clark, the much beloved stage and screen comedian (originally with partner Paul McCullough, and later as a solo), had so much difficulty adjusting to television that his gig as one of the original hosts of the *Comedy Hour* ended after only four appearances.

But within the next few years, television became crowded with the top comedians of the day, from both radio and silver screen. It then surpassed both by becoming *the* desirable medium for comedy—a medium that could reach millions of viewers, and produce millions of laughs, instantaneously. It's little wonder that radio comedians began to abandon their visually-challenged medium in favor of the glass tube that could carry their faces, as well as their voices, into America's living rooms. In the interest of sustaining their careers, they really had little choice.

Still more members of the "old school" of comedy jumped on the TV bandwagon the following season. Red Skelton joined their ranks almost thirty years after first befriending Ed on that street corner in Vincennes. Skelton had enjoyed a decade of success with his radio program, and in films, before making a smooth transition to TV. He brought with him his assortment of regular characters, and, being a true master of pantomime comedy in the purest clown tradition, thrived in the setting that allowed him to perform heavily visual pieces. Of all the comedians who began their TV careers in

the 1950-51 season, Skelton's program would last the longest—a full twenty years.

The irony at the time was that radio, which so seriously wounded vaudeville in the mid-1920s by becoming a valued fixture in virtually every home in America, was itself now in trouble. It had slipped a notch on the mass entertainment food chain, and was being quite literally devoured by television.

Chapter 11: Out with the Old . . .

> *"At the top of his early success he martyred himself over his family. When his second round of fame ended, he was martyred by the nature of this new kind of show business, and he was left washed up on the beach."*
> —Keenan Wynn on Ed

Ed's lighter work schedule on *Four Star Revue* enabled him to take a role unlike any he had played before. In 1951, he became the voice of Mad Hatter in Disney's animated feature, *Alice In Wonderland*. It was a role perfectly suited to his voice and quirky inflections. In the Mad Hatter's featured scene, the tea party, Ed and Bob Hope sidekick Jerry Colonna sing a spirited duet on a number called "The Unbirthday Song." Here the Mad Hatter and the March Hare explain to Alice that for the one birthday each of us has every year, we also have 364 *un*birthdays. As was a common practice among Disney animators, they gave the Mad Hatter a definite resemblance to Ed, with a bulbous nose and thick tufts of hair sticking out from under each side of his top hat.

The film was released in late July. Film critic Bosley Crowther in The New York Times wrote, "The fabulous Mad Hatter, while a wonderfully lunatic clown, giggles and chirps in the familiar and inseparable voice of Ed Wynn. The March Hare, as crazy as the Hatter, is Jerry Colonna to the ear. The mind's eye beholds these two comedians, rather than the unique conceits of Mr. Carroll." Film historian Leonard Maltin has described Ed and Colonna's contributions as "hilarious," adding, "What one remembers specifically about the Tea Party are those two delightful voices, and the 'Unbirthday Song,' more than the visuals..."

The second season of *Four Star Revue* began in the fall of 1951 with a title change to *All-Star Revue*, in acknowledgement of its growing roster of rotating hosts. Martha Raye, Olsen & Johnson, Spike Jones, Victor Borge, Bob Hope, the Ritz Brothers, and Paul Winchell all hosted at least one episode that season.

In November, completion of the highly anticipated transcontinental cable opened a new era in American broadcasting, by allowing programs to be aired live from coast to coast. This enabled *All Star Revue* to move out of the Center Theatre and to Los Angeles, which was then aspiring to become the center of the TV industry, as it had done with motion pictures. It also hastened the immigration of homesick Hollywood stars, including Ed, from the New York TV studios back to L.A.

Perhaps the most surprising casualty of the transcontinental cable was New York's Center Theatre. In October of 1953, only three years after so much money had been spent to convert the venue into a showcase TV studio, it was announced that the facility would be demolished.

But television in 1951 was expanding almost *too* quickly for Hollywood to keep pace. The sudden wave of new programs and stars, defying earlier expectations of a more gradual move from East to West, caught the networks somewhat ill prepared. A shortage of proper production facilities sent network executives searching to find and purchase spare movie lots and unused soundstages, and even to commandeer the studios of their local L.A. affiliates on occasion. Their counterparts at the networks' headquarters in New York reportedly had, to that point, deliberately dragged their feet developing TV production facilities in Hollywood, in order to allow New York to maintain its broadcasting supremacy. But, once the cable was completed, they did not anticipate the swiftness with which the industry would expand to the West Coast. Only ABC had begun preparations early, by taking over the aging, twenty-three acre Vitagraph movie lot for conversion to television.

The March 8, 1952 *All-Star Revue* broadcast included a surprise for Ed. Among his guests that night were Edward Arnold and Jimmy Durante. Ed sang a few songs with Durante, such as "Shine on Harvest Moon." As was his custom to close each show by ambling onstage in his nightshirt and going to bed, this time the cast and guests surprised him with an anniversary cake in honor of his fiftieth year in show business. Arnold also presented an award to Ed from the Actor's Equity.

All Star Revue re-tooled that summer, which included making changes in the cast. Ed was among those not invited to return. The show retained only Durante from original rotation, while new regulars were added.

It was especially unfortunate that Ed had been dropped from the airwaves during the very season that offered the greatest number of comedy stars to be seen on television. In retrospect, it is nothing short of astounding that TV viewers, in the fall of 1952, had the opportunity to watch, on a *weekly* basis, a veritable Who's Who of stellar comedians starring on sitcoms or hosting variety shows. Imagine skimming through a copy of the *TV Guide* at the time, and finding among the listings:

SUNDAY: *The Colgate Comedy Hour* (rotating hosts: Eddie Cantor, Abbott & Costello, Martin & Lewis), *The Red Skelton Show*

MONDAY: *I Love Lucy* (Lucille Ball)

TUESDAY: *The Red Buttons Show*, *Texaco Star Theater* (Milton Berle)

WEDNESDAY: *I Married Joan* (Joan Davis)

THURSDAY: *The George Burns & Gracie Allen Show*, *You Bet Your Life* (Groucho Marx)

FRIDAY: *Our Miss Brooks* (Eve Arden)

SATURDAY: *The Jackie Gleason Show*, *Your Show of Shows* (Sid Caesar)

All in one week—*every* week, in the autumn of 1952.

Upon being released from his contract, Ed was left without a regular gig on TV, or anywhere else. But he would manage to stay in the public eye, as a guest on a myriad of programs, throughout the next few years.

In June of 1953, Ed had the dubious honor of being surprised by Ralph Edwards for an episode of *This Is Your Life*. It was often the case with this program that the celebrity guest of honor did not necessarily appreciate being ambushed and seeing his or her life reviewed by the unctuous Edwards (who said everything through his relentless smile). Laurel & Hardy, for instance, were known to have felt infuriated by being "caught" on the show, since they were accustomed to preparing carefully for each and every public appearance. Ed wasn't much happier about his own turn as guest. The best the program could do in the way of surprise guests were members of his own family and a handful of obscure vaudevillians. Keenan later reported that Ed was especially upset by being presented as a has-been, regardless of the program's good intentions.

Some of Ed's potential projects at the time never got past the talking stage. In the spring of '53, he spoke of his plans to star in a film called *Wonder Kid* with Keenan, in which he was to play Keenan's son. But the film was never made.

That September, an intriguing plan emerged for Ed to host a new TV audience participation show, and made it as far as the audition stage for CBS. Cartoonist Rube Goldberg, famous for his sketches of bizarre and comical contraptions, signed a deal with the network to contribute sketches of his devices, which would then be constructed for real on the show. Ed, as host, would have audience members attempt to try out the contraptions. CBS executive Harry Ackerman promised the format "will give TV something never tried before." But upon auditioning the show for the network, the idea apparently proved more promising in concept than in practice, and never made it to air.

In January of 1954, Ed appeared as a cameo guest on *The Ed Sullivan Show* twice in January alone. For the first one, he was shown standing in the wings backstage waiting to do a trapeze act, with Sullivan explaining that there wouldn't be time for him that week. The following week, viewers saw Ed still waiting backstage for his chance to go on, only to hear the same excuse from Sullivan, with apologies.

On April 18, he appeared as the celebrity mystery guest on the popular game show *What's My Line?* On each week's program, the panelists (Arlene Francis, Steve Allen, critic Dorothy Kilgallen, and publisher Bennett Cerf) would don blindfolds before asking the mystery guest a string of yes-or-no questions, and the guest would disguise his or her voice while giving the answers. However, Ed's voice was so recognizable that, after signing in on the blackboard to great applause, he brought a violin with him to his seat. He dragged the bow across a high-pitched string for a "yes" answer, and across a lower note string for a "no" answer (panelist Bennett Cerf suspected that Ed was the guest before the questioning began, and promptly disqualified himself). The segment was full of fun, but the panelists' many probing questions weren't helping them figure out his identity. Finally, Ed dispensed with the violin and answered a single question in his poorly-disguised voice. Not surprisingly, the panel immediately figured out who he was.

He made still more TV guest appearances throughout the year. September brought the first of what would ultimately total seven visits to *The Red Skelton Show,* and he appeared on *The George Gobel Show* just before Christmas. His sporadic appearances continued throughout 1954 and 1955, when he visited *The Ed Sullivan Show* again, as well as the game show *The Name's The Same.*

Television audiences were always glad to see Ed, considering how such a large swath of the population had grown up either seeing him onstage or hearing him as the Fire Chief. And even the younger viewers could have recalled seeing his original TV variety show. But the truth was that Ed's career as a comedy headliner had been dying a slow death since he was dismissed from *All-Star Revue.* Despite his virtually bottomless reservoir of gags, props, and costumes, his audiences had come to know almost all of them throughout the previous forty years. Even the jokes they *hadn't* heard before may have sounded vaguely familiar. Ed had entertained his audiences through a Great Depression, Prohibition, two World Wars, and now a Cold War. The world was constantly changing to be sure. Alas, his comedy was not. And, while it was difficult to argue with the long-term success of his comedic *modus operandi*, by the mid-1950s the world had simply changed too much for his funny hats and oversized shoes to generate waves of laughter.

His heyday as one of the funniest clowns in show business was in danger of receding in the memories of his audiences. And watching his own illustrious career slowly fade out filled him with confusion and depression. He was approaching 70, and while the idea of retirement would appeal to most men of that age, he couldn't stomach the thought. "If a man has been an office worker or has worked at a machine all his life," he said, "he's probably tired. And if he's tired he should retire. But I'm an active man. This is an exciting profession. I've got to feel I'm giving pleasure to an audience or I'm not happy myself."

So, in November of 1954, he appeared onstage once again, but this time headlining a bill for a Las Vegas gig, in the Romona Room of the Hotel Last Frontier. There were no surprises to be found in the act. While one review described Ed as both "durable" and "lovable," it also grumbled about how he "goes through his familiar half dozen changes of ridiculous costumes and keeps springing the corny jokes that used to go over big." And he was once again chastised for indulging in an old habit when he interrupted singer June Roselle's aria from *Tosca*, "to the point where the audience is almost in revolt." Keenan spoke of seeing Ed perform in the Vegas show on his 68th birthday. "He was using pickups from his old acts. It looked old-fashioned. The public was saying, 'Oh, isn't that nice?' It was like saying, 'You should have seen him when.'"

Life on the home front at the time was no kinder. Dorothy filed for divorce in February of 1955, with the charge of "extreme cruelty" (the cruelty being emotional rather than physical). She stated that her husband "felt his profession was very important to him, and he was unwilling to spend any time with me at social gatherings." The divorce became final a month later. The alimony arrangement cost him half of his assets and twenty-five percent of whatever he was to earn in the future. Ed had little choice but to put his Beverly Hills house on the market, and move into a rented apartment on Wilshire Boulevard. The end of this, his third marriage (for reasons strikingly similar to those of the previous two), left him feeling alone and that much more eager to find work. "When I wasn't working," he said, "I'd get a little ache here and a little pain there. I want to die working."

By early 1956, with the flow of requests for his presence on TV reduced to a trickle, he felt forgotten and unwanted by the very business he loved so much. "After 53 years, I couldn't get any work," he later explained. "The Big Curtain seemed to have rung down. George Gobel called me once, Red Skelton once, Ed Sullivan had me come to New York for his show. That's all. I couldn't understand what was happening to me; I thought I had a reputation in this business." He was deeply hurt, and fearful that his half-century of bringing laughter to so many people had, ultimately, gone unappreciated.

The moment came one day when Ed called Keenan to bemoan the shortage of job offers coming his way. Keenan then invited his father to stop by the house for a talk.

To Ed's surprise, Keenan served up an unexpected helping of tough love—with an emphasis on the tough. As reluctant as he was to offer advice, since he himself resisted any and all career assistance from Ed, Keenan felt he needed to set his father straight about a few things. The vaudeville clown style of comedy, he said, was looking terribly antiquated in 1956, and Ed was in danger of having his audiences laugh at his gags more out of a sense of nostalgia than anything else. He suggested that Ed had two choices: retire, or try his hand at drama. In truth, there wasn't really much of a choice at all, as Ed never considered retirement as an option. "I thought it was darned good advice to change, and that I'd best try drama. I'd never spoken a straight line in my life, but Keenan was very reassuring. He said, 'I think you'd be good, because in the living room you're the saddest guy I've ever seen.'"

Now that father and son agreed that Ed should try his hand at drama, they needed the right role for him. They met with his agent, Kurt Frings, who then spoke with Keenan's close friend, actor/director Jose Ferrer. Ferrer was still casting for a film drama he was directing, called *The Great Man*. The story centers on radio reporter Joe Harris (to be played by Ferrer) who, after the death of a popular but mean-spirited radio broadcaster named Herb Fuller, is assigned to produce a memorial program. But he discovers that those who knew Fuller personally couldn't think of a kind thing to say about him.

Keenan was to have a role in the film, as Fuller's producer (the name of the story's fictitious Amalgamated Network must have given Ed a chill). And Kurt Frings' suggestion that Ed might be able to handle a dramatic part interested Ferrer, who had a relatively small role in mind for him. The part of Paul Beaseley, the owner of a small town radio station who gave Fuller his start, was basically a 1,400-word monologue. Still, it was the furthest thing Ed could have imagined undertaking professionally.

His misgivings about playing drama were well-founded. To accomplish the task, his entire mindset as an entertainer had to be drastically adjusted. "I was as scared as a kid going on his first audition," he said of his first meeting with Ferrer. After studying his part for the film and coming back to perform the monologue for the director, Ed awaited Ferrer's assessment. Ferrer decided Ed still had much work to do. They went through laborious rehearsals together right up to the first of three days scheduled for shooting the scene. But when it came time to perform his part before the cameras, Ed did so without a hitch, in one take. Ferrer, moved to tears, yelled, "Cut!" and jumped off his stool to embrace Ed. "That's all. Go home," he said. Keenan, who had been watching the scene, stepped forward to give his father a kiss as well. Word quickly spread that Ed had turned in a remarkable performance—especially for a novice.

Upon the film's release, kudos poured in. *Variety* reported, "Ed Wynn is outstanding as the pious owner of a small New England radio station who gave the 'morning man' his start."

For his first dramatic effort, he not only received a Golden Globe nomination for Best Supporting Actor, but also a BAFTA (British Academy of Film And Television Arts) nomination for Best Foreign Actor.

He may have scored an unexpected personal and professional victory, but his success also had the effect of giving him a sudden and somewhat inflated sense of his skills as an actor. Ed caught the acting bug, all right, but he also suffered from its feverish side effect.

His next dramatic role, in Rod Serling's *Requiem for a Heavyweight*, would actually be the first the public would see of the re-invented Ed Wynn, since it was scheduled to air before *The Great Man*'s release date.

Serling's story of a washed-up boxer and his seedy, exploitative manager was only the second production under the *Playhouse 90* banner. Keenan landed the role of Maish, the desperate, debt-ridden manager of Mountain McClintock, played by Jack Palance. Ed was hired to play Army, the trainer who uses his ringside skills to keep Mountain on his feet against increasingly younger and stronger opponents. Ralph Nelson directed the program.

Producer Martin Manulis wanted Ed for the part of Army regardless of the misgivings expressed by almost everyone else involved in the show. "That was a push of mine, to have Ed in," Manulis recalled. "But I knew him because I was a friend of Keenan's, and I knew Ed as a friend." Manulis also admitted to another motivation in casting Ed: stunt casting could only help ratings for the new anthology series. "We had to do interesting things with casting. We tried to beef up things with actors who were getting a shot at something they didn't get elsewhere." Ed received $7,500 for his work on the show.

Keenan, for one, wasn't happy about playing opposite his father, and not only due to Ed's inexperience as a dramatic actor (his successful performance in *The Great Man* notwithstanding). Keenan feared it would pull him back into the "Ed Wynn's son" territory he had been so determined to escape for most of his life.

As for Ed, he faced his own daunting new challenge, one totally alien to anything he had ever undertaken in his fifty years as an entertainer. Memorizing a single dramatic speech for *The Great Man* was one thing—but exchanging lines with other actors, blocking his movements, and doing both at the same time—on live television—was quite another.

"The first thing I had to do was unlearn everything I've done for half a century," he said. "If you think that's easy, try it. For instance, I've a scene in which I cry emotionally. I went home and practiced in front of a mirror. I was so funny, I got hysterical. Try as I might, I unconsciously tended to make it comic. That's fifty-four years of training asserting itself."

Keenan's concerns were somewhat vindicated when it became evident that Ed's rehearsals were not going well. Manulis found himself fielding an increasing number of complaints not only from Keenan, but from Rod Serling and Ralph Nelson as well.

"At one point Keenan came to me and said, 'You've got to fire the old man, we can't go on with him.' I said, 'Well, he looks pretty good to me.' He said, 'He can't remember anything in rehearsal, and when he doesn't remember, he does his schtick...' I was just not gonna have it. Finally, they all really ganged together—Sterling, and Ralph Nelson...Serling threatened to take his name off the credits if Ed wasn't fired.

"I said to Keenan, 'How can you do this? You're out to destroy your father.' He said, 'No, he's gonna destroy *me*, because I have a lot of scenes with him, and I'm not gonna be able to do them. I'll be trying to hold him up.' I said, 'Can you just worry about yourself?'

The situation began to look so dire that Manulis and casting director Ethel Winant instructed Ned Glass, who had a small role as a bartender, to study Ed's lines. Glass watched all of the rehearsals so that he knew Ed's part as well as his own. Ethel arranged for him to stand by just in case—behind the bar, under a couch, or wherever he would be able to discreetly keep track of Ed's performance, in case of an emergency, i.e. Ed going totally blank live on TV. Ed was unaware of this, and didn't think twice about seeing Glass at rehearsals.

Having secretly arranged for Glass to be ready to literally step into Ed's role at the first sign of trouble, Manulis visited the rehearsals on the set to get a feel for how things were progressing—*if* they were progressing.

> "I really was quite surprised. The show was really damn good, and I thought that Ed was quite all right! He did forget his lines a couple of times, but he didn't do his giggle or anything, he just forgot. But he was very nervous about being there. When the thing ended...I said to everybody, 'It's a wonderful show. You're gonna have a huge hit, it's just wonderful.'"

Manulis then went to Ed and said, "Ed, in all these years I never could believe you could do this. It's so good, so wonderful, I'm so glad I know you, and got you to do this." He then retreated to his office, careful not to make eye contact with the others.

"I trusted the fact that an old pro, however wrong he was for the part, would pull up at show time...I don't think he knew that it had gotten to the point where they wanted to fire him. I don't think so."

Ed may not have known about the back-up plan to have Glass at the ready, but there were still other difficulties to overcome throughout rehearsals. It was feared that his lisp could become a distraction during the more dramatic scenes. He had nervous hands as well, due to the early stages of Parkinson's Disease. Director Nelson explained, "We had to devise tricks. To control the lisp, we took out a lot of words with 's' sounds. To control the hands, we had him play solitaire during one important scene, and hold boxing gloves in another...We began to see that we might get away with it. He was humble and patient about everything. And he was far better than we thought he could be."

Ed did make noticeable progress in rehearsals as the live broadcast neared, but that didn't negate a last-minute attack of nerves. Red Skelton, at the studio for a wardrobe fitting, saw Ed at a particularly vulnerable moment during a break in rehearsals. He caught sight of Ed sitting in a car in the lot, looking scared to death, and drunk—a rarity for him.

"Ed, what's the matter?" Skelton asked. "I can't go on and do this," Ed said. " I'm not going on." Skelton stayed with him all day, helping fill Ed with coffee.

Requiem aired live on the evening of October 6. After all of the strife that hung heavy over the rehearsals, Ed turned in a flawless, word-perfect performance. Ironically, it was Keenan who, while keeping such a watchful eye on his father, fluffed one of his own lines.

All told, the acting by each and every cast member in *Requiem* was nothing short of brilliant, and Manulis' confidence in Ed paid off. "He did come up, way up, and he was very good. He certainly didn't let the show down in any way, and I think the old man must have gone through hell, because you can feel that there's dissention going on.

"And people were thrilled to see him—he was a *famous* comedian—the Fire Chief and everything—he had a huge audience of people who loved him. Maybe someone else would have played it with bigger nuance or whatever, but this served our purpose very well."

Skelton sent a telegram to Ed with a little inside joke: "Ed, you were wonderful, but remember—just do comedy."

As soon as the show ended, cast and crew rushed over to Ed for a round of congratulations. Ed later recalled, "Keenan threw his arms around me and hugged me. It was like an opening night on Broadway after the curtain goes down. I guess the old man surprised them." But as Keenan stepped back from the group of well-wishers patting his father on the back, he was heard to say to himself, "Here I am, Ed Wynn's son again."

Chapter 12: A Star Is Reborn

> *"It's just remarkable...If I were younger, I'd be swell-headed. I've been through that too. I was younger once and I was swell-headed. But I passed 70 last November and now I can only be grateful."*
> —Ed Wynn, 1957

When the Emmy nominations for the season were announced, Ed's name was among those nominated in the Best Supporting Actor category. With this addition to his resume (the winner that year, before Drama and Comedy were divided into separate categories, was Carl Reiner for *Caesar's Hour*), he found himself receiving offers for a wide range of parts, both in feature films and for guest roles on TV dramas.

Keenan, nearly two decades after Ed's first successes as a character actor, offered this assessment of how his father was able to make the transition from clown to dramatic actor: "For his last ten years, he was a very fine actor because a clown is an actor. A comedian is not an actor. I wish all of us could do what, say, Jack Benny does, or what Bob Hope does. But basically they are comedians. A great clown can make you cry. A comedian can make you laugh, and that's it. He will not play on your emotions."

Such an assessment is open to endless debate with regards to the differences, if any, between a comic, a clown, and a comedian, or which has the better inherent potential to be a good dramatic actor. But such a debate is best left for another day.

In hindsight, Ed embarked on his new acting career at the right time—not just on a personal or even professional level, but because by the midway point of the 1950s, significant cracks had appeared in the comedy world's facade. It was not a good time to be a veteran comedian on television, or anywhere else.

This was especially true in the case of the movies. Throughout the entire decade of the 1950s, motion picture comedy suffered from a virtual drought of creativity and a woeful shortage of familiar, big-name comedy stars in major studio productions. History began to repeat itself. Just as the almost magnetic attraction of films and radio pulled vaudevillians in the 1930s off the stage and put them in front of microphones and movie cameras, television in the early 1950s exerted its own irresistible influence on performers—in some cases those very same former vaudevillians. Of course, entertainers weren't obliged to choose one medium in which to work at the exclusion of the others. But for comedians, even for those skeptics who had misgivings about their own odds for success, television represented the future. As they abandoned radio with TV's rise to dominance, movies suffered an even greater comedy vacuum.

Exacerbating the sorry state of film comedy at the time was the fact that many veteran movie comedians who did *not* turn their attention to television simply left the film industry outright, leaving a void simply too big to fill. By the end of 1950, the motion picture industry found itself without all of its true comedy giants, such as W.C. Fields (who died in 1946), Buster Keaton, Charlie Chaplin, Harold Lloyd, the Marx Brothers, and Laurel & Hardy. The resulting dearth of feature film comedies throughout the decade provided a shocking contrast to what had been produced by the major movie studios in the preceding twenty years.

Specifically: The Marx Brothers ended their movie career with their last film together, *Love Happy*, released in March of 1950. This swan song was only their 13th film in twenty years. Groucho had by then lost his enthusiasm for making films. He was riding high as the host of the quiz show *You Bet Your Life*, which was soon to make a successful transition from radio to TV. Harpo had cut his own workload considerably, but made numerous guest appearances on television (including his famous visit to *I Love Lucy*). Chico popped up on TV occasionally, with and without his brothers, sometimes leading a big band.

Laurel & Hardy, after making a handful of inferior comedies for an uncaring 20th Century Fox studio, released their own disastrous final film in 1950, *Atoll K*, which was made in Europe with a confused, multi-national, multi-lingual production team, and with a very ill Stan Laurel. After Stan recovered, he and Ollie resumed their career, most notably with a British stage tour, but they had left their movie days behind them.

As for comedy's other elder statesmen of the screen, Charlie Chaplin offered only two features in the 1950s—*Limelight* in 1952, and *A King In New York* in 1957. His friend/rival Buster Keaton enjoyed a new lease on life on television (much to Chaplin's chagrin), starring for a time on his own program, and in numerous commercials. Abbott and Costello's films, wildly popular throughout the 1940s, suffered a steady decline in quality after 1950, as they too turned more of their attention to television. They began their stint as rotating hosts of the *Colgate Comedy Hour* in 1951, and starred in their own half-hour sitcom in 1952.

Even the Three Stooges' comedy suffered throughout the 1950s, first from the loss of Curly Howard, who was forced to retire after a stroke in 1946 (he died in 1952). Shemp Howard dutifully stepped in for his brother, but despite his considerable comic abilities, his films with the Stooges did not have the comic impact as Curly's had. Shemp died in 1955. His replacements, Joe Besser, and later, Joe DeRita, joined too late in the game to make much of their own mark on the franchise. More significantly, Columbia Studios, the Stooges' home for a quarter-century, closed its short subject division in 1958, and chose not to renew the team's contract.

All of these developments led to such a meager output of feature film comedies throughout the 1950s that it's possible count on one hand the quality comedies produced by major American studios in that decade. Only *Born Yesterday, The Seven Year Itch, Mister Roberts, Pillow Talk, Operation Petticoat* (Blake Edwards' directorial debut) and Billy Wilder's much revered *Some Like It Hot* have demonstrated any staying power in the years since their release.

But even these films did not star established *comedians*, but rather light comic actors—Judy Holliday, Rock Hudson, Doris Day, Tony Randall, Jack Lemmon—similar to how the screwball comedies of the 1930s starred the likes of Carole Lombard, Claudette Colbert, William Powell, and Cary Grant. It wasn't difficult to see that the true Golden Age of film comedy, led by the titans of the art form, was quickly receding into the distant past. In 1960, Bosley Crowther, film critic for *The New York Times*, lamented how true slapstick, so popular in the silent comedy classics of the 1920s (and revived via tribute films such as *When Comedy Was King*, compiled by producer Robert Youngston), had given way to bland, suburban comedies like *Please Don't Eat The Daisies*. "Considering the pallid quality of most screen comedy these days," he wrote, "it is gladdening but saddening, we must tell you, to look at *When Comedy Was King*."

Even as television continued to gain viewers and strengthen its influence on popular culture, life wasn't looking very rosy behind the scenes at most TV network comedy programs. In June of 1956, *The New York Times* printed a curious piece in which television comedy writers were invited to speak their minds about their jobs and their bosses, under the protection of anonymity. With that assurance, they offered these thoughts:

> "Most comedians are highly neurotic egomaniacs who would ruin a script to satisfy their own insecurities."

> "A comedian (I have written for most of them) is usually an insecure and frightened man. The more contact he has with his writers, the more confidence he is apt to have in the script. The end result is to make the writer's work easier."

> "Most comedians are not qualified judges of the kind of material they should use."

> "There are a lot of poor comedy writers with whom the comic should not confer and a lot of poor comedians to whom the writer would be better off not talking."

Another major loss for comedy at the time occurred with the break-up of Martin & Lewis in 1956, almost exactly ten years after they first became a team. They had been the darlings of the entertainment world, complementing their successful film career (where they became the country's #1 box office attraction), with legendary nightclub stage shows and rollicking sketches as rotating hosts of *The Colgate Comedy Hour*. But Dean, growing weary of Jerry's onstage antics—which at times interfered with Dean's earnest attempts to sing—decided it was time for the two to go their separate ways.

Later that same year, Abbott & Costello—considerably older than Martin & Lewis, and just as tired of each other's company—released their final film together, *Dance With Me, Henry*. The team split up shortly thereafter, after twenty years of success in every mass medium in existence.

The remaining few years of the decade saw troubles for television comedy as well as film. The creative decline of Berle, and the departures of both Caesar and Gleason from weekly television dealt a big blow. They had appeared to run out of steam—if only temporarily—from the grind of producing weekly comedy-variety, and from overseeing each and every aspect of their respective shows. In Caesar's case, the ever-changing face of television introduced the biggest threat yet to *Caesar's Hour*. Mild mannered accordionist Lawrence Welk unexpectedly grabbed a sizable share of the comedian's audience, causing ratings for *Caesar's Hour* to drop. The quality of the show, however, did not. In fact, the program won five Emmys just months before its cancellation in 1957. In Gleason's case, his famous ego got the better of him when he demanded a pay raise that CBS refused to grant.

By the spring of '57, *Caesar's Hour* was about to leave the air for good, *The Colgate Comedy Hour* and *All-Star Revue* were long gone. *Berle's Buick Show* ended the previous June, and Ernie Kovacs' visually innovative show would be off the air by September. With all of this, the state of comedy had grown so dire that *Life* magazine, in its April, 1957 issue (featuring Kovacs on the cover) described a "comedy crisis" that had descended upon television. "Good laughs—rich, full-bellied yoks and boffs—are also currently hard to find on the Broadway stage, in nightclubs, on radio and at the movies."

There were still more developments that did not bode well for comedy on television as the decade neared its end. Gracie Allen retired from show business permanently in 1958. George Burns attempted to carry on without her in a revamped TV show, but that effort lasted a single season. Lou Costello, who had been enjoying life as a frequent TV guest without Bud Abbott, died in 1959. He was only 52 years old.

In addition, the face of TV programming had been undergoing a major change. The tube had fostered the growth of another genre, the Western—and with such success that by the late '50s Westerns had utterly dominated the airwaves. More than *two dozen* Westerns had squeezed their way onto the networks' prime time schedules by the end of the decade, leaving precious little room for comedy, or much of anything else.

There was yet another factor determining the passing of Ed's brand of comedy. By the late 1950s, as sketch comedians and vaudeville-style comics saw their fortunes wane, a new generation of comedians caught the fancy of the public. A stand-up comedy revolution took shape in big city nightclubs, especially on the East and West coasts. Even the standard term "monologist" was giving way to the term "stand-up." New York clubs, such as The Bitter End and Cafe Wha? became the breeding ground in which a new wave of satirical comedians began to thrive. This new style of comedian didn't wear baggy pants and oversized shoes, but rather a business suit and tie, and stood center stage, with few or no props, and regaled audiences with satire, observational comedy, or improvisation. Routines incorporated current events, politics, and social trends. It was a more contemporary, verbal, and cerebral comedy than the slapstick-heavy sketch comedy and well-worn patter so dominant in vaudeville and on early television, and the better comedians' efforts were rewarded with fast-growing legions of followers.

Television itself can be credited in no small way for this shift in tastes. With nightly news programs and documentaries bringing world events into living rooms across the nation, television gave the public a more immediate connection with all that was transpiring across America and elsewhere, and in a manner that movie theatre newsreels couldn't do. The faces of presidents, congressmen, and world leaders, and images of conflicts on city streets and distant battlefields, had become much more real and recognizable even to television viewers. This enabled comedians on stage to drop names and refer to events they knew their audiences had probably seen on television that same week. Of course, not all of the new stand-ups were social satirists commenting on the news of the day. Comedy styles were divided roughly into two camps. There were the comedians who kept a keen eye on the world, and who used events to sharpen their humor with varying degrees of cynicism, even anger (Lenny Bruce, Mort Sahl). Then there were the more conventional, good-natured performers who played it for laughs, but kept it all relatively genteel and inoffensive (Bob Newhart, Shelley Berman, Jonathan Winters, Nichols & May). They also did not rely on teams of writers for most of their material, as had those comedians of Bob Hope and Eddie Cantor's ilk. One thing was certain: the day of the mother-in-law joke was fast approaching twilight. And, as this young generation of comedians took comedy in a new direction, they left the likes of Ed and his vaudevillian peers looking downright antiquated.

Ed may have been almost agonizingly slow to acknowledge the passing of his style of comedy, but at least he can be commended for staying true to himself and not attempting to emulate the new mode making the rounds. His one-time TV rival Milton Berle gave himself a comedy make-over, causing his own career considerable harm.

Berle's initial burst of success on TV was relatively short-lived. Despite his enormous impact on television in 1948, he discovered within a few years that his broad, boisterous style of slapstick was losing favor with television audiences. Over-saturation and changing tastes had combined to nudge him out of the spotlight. He attempted a new format for his program (with Buick as his new sponsor), and, more dramatically, toned down his outrageous image, favoring conservative business suits over his clownish costumes. He soon regretted it.

"I had violated one of my basic rules of work," Berle confessed. "For years I had told new young comics that they had to decide on their own personal image before they worked, and that they must never violate that image in the public's mind. But when I...turned the aggressive, pushy 'Milton Berle' into a passive straight man for the *Buick* format, I had broken my image and hurt myself, even when the ratings went up."

Ed continued to appear as a guest on TV variety programs, such as Jack Benny's and Kate Smith's. But to truly extend his career, there was little left for him to do other than take the fateful

180-degree turn away from his comic persona and delve further into drama.

His first leading dramatic role on television was "The Great American Hoax," an installment of *The 20th Century-Fox Hour*. The story's theme about the mandatory retirement age of sixty-five struck a chord with Ed. "The theme was so close to me," he said, "that I couldn't bring myself to turn it down. Not that I look back with any bitterness…I hope I have proven something by starting a whole new career at 69."

Yet another dramatic role came that May, on NBC's *Alcoa Hour* drama, "The Protege."

He continued to speak in interviews of how the transition to his new life as an actor wasn't as easy as it appeared. His successful dramatic performances to date—in *Requiem* and *The Great Man*—required the same kind of monumental effort on his part that it would require for a right-handed person to suddenly begin writing with his left hand. For Ed, he literally had to use a different part of his brain. "This transition has caused quite a mental upheaval," he said. " If every time you've left the dressing room to go on stage, you wore funny hats and clothes—well, suddenly after fifty-four years to come out and be a human being—that gives me a good deal of apprehension." While posing for publicity shots for *The Protege*, he also realized that he was having the first straight pictures taken of him in over 30 years.

"There's a place in [the story] where the character is to do a bit of comedy. Someone suggested that bit be old Ed Wynn. I said, no, I shouldn't do 'Ed Wynn' while being someone else. Maybe I'll have to create a new comedy style for it—but not the shoes, not the old Ed Wynn."

He may not have fully appreciated the significance of that decision at the time, but it signaled one of the major turning points of his career, and of his life. And it was not so different from a decision made almost thirty years earlier by one of his comedy contemporaries, Charlie Chaplin.

Chaplin developed his "Little Tramp" character not long after he left the stage to begin his career as a film comedian in 1914. For the next fifteen years, in nearly eighty films, he expressed his philosophy, his emotions, and his comic inventiveness through the tramp. And, of course, in the process, he became one of the most recognizable faces in the world.

But the advent of talkies became a source of great anxiety for Chaplin. He hated the very concept of sound films, dreaded their arrival, and faced their takeover of the film industry with a sense of genuine panic. While his fellow comedians were eager to be a part of the new sound era, Chaplin tried to cling to the silents. He kept a brave face and insisted that his pantomime skills were immune to the sound revolution, but in truth he simply could not figure out how his tramp character would speak on film. Moreover, he wasn't so sure if the tramp *should* speak on film. He found himself faced with what he considered a no-win situation, and pondered whether sound film would mean the end of his career. He had created and lived with his one character, and knew him inside and out. The only thing he couldn't bring himself to create for the tramp was a voice.

"Occasionally I mused over the possibility of making a sound film," Chaplin wrote in his autobiography, "but the thought sickened me, for I realized I could never achieve the excellence of my silent pictures. It would mean giving up my tramp character entirely. Some people suggested that the tramp might talk. This was unthinkable, for the first word he ever uttered would transform him into another person." So, without affording his Little Tramp character the opportunity to speak, he saw his film career as essentially over. He even once confided to Groucho Marx, "I wish I could talk on screen the way you do."

Jump ahead a quarter-century, and we find the great clown Ed Wynn arriving at a very similar crossroads, choosing to retire his own beloved comedy character only out of necessity. In doing so, he demonstrated that he had finally acknowledged that the Perfect Fool belonged to another time.

Ed was not the first accomplished comedian to achieve success as a dramatic actor. Chaplin created heartbreaking drama in *The Kid* and *City Lights*. Jack Benny played it mostly straight, to great effect, in *To Be or Not to Be*. The great Carole Lombard, who began her film career taking pies in the face for Mack Sennett, starred in classic 1930s screwball comedies such as *My Man Godfrey* and *Nothing Sacred*. But she also took on convincing dramatic roles, alternating between slapstick comedies and melodramas with remarkable ease, and as few actresses have done in the decades since her death.

Groucho Marx wrote, "There's is hardly a comedian alive who isn't capable of doing a first-rate dramatic role. But there are mighty few dramatic actors who could essay a comic role with any distinction...All first-rate comedians who have played dramatic roles are almost unanimous in saying that compared to being funny, dramatic acting is like a two-week vacation in the country."

Years later, Jerry Lewis concurred: "The hard job is doing comedy. That's what's rough. Acting is a snap, but acting for an *actor* is hard work...because that's all he does. It *is* like two weeks in the country. Christ, that's a pleasure, and easy...that's nowhere as naked as being a comedian."

Despite the effectiveness with which Ed set aside his beloved alter ego to pursue a dramatic career, he disagreed with Groucho's assertion that there was a connection between a comedian's talent to make people laugh, and the ability to dovetail that talent into dramatic acting. "They are altogether different," he insisted. "As the Perfect Fool, I wasn't a real persona at all. I was a caricature...The Perfect Fool couldn't sit down at the table and dine with a family. He had on a funny hat and his face was made up crazy and his mind didn't run along ordinary channels. He couldn't hold a normal conversation with anybody because he wasn't interested in anybody.

"As a dramatic actor, you have to sit down and communicate with other people in terms that have been rigidly set for you by the writer and director. You have to relate to them as one human being to another."

Now that he was a hot item as an actor, Ed was honored in a one-hour installment of *Texaco Command Appearance* on September 19, 1957. Steve Allen hosted, with guests including English music hall legend Beatrice Lillie, and singer Janet Blair. Reviews were mixed. *Billboard* described the event as a "warm, bubbly, graceful tribute to the 55-year career of Ed Wynn" with a script that "deftly avoided mush." But *The New York Times*, while extolling Ed's genuine charm and gentle humor in the brief segments he was actually on center stage, saw the show as merely an excuse to showcase the other performers. "What a pity that the producers of *Command*

Appearance did not let their guest put on more of the show; his was the experienced hand."

On November 17, Ed starred in the *Hallmark Television Playhouse* adaptation of "On Borrowed Time," playing Gramps Northrup. He shared the screen with Claude Rains and Margaret Hamilton. In the story, Gramps wards off death to keep his young grandson from being raised by a nasty aunt (Hamilton) "As the understanding Gramps," Jack Gould of *The New York Times* wrote, "Mr. Wynn added to his roster of expert character portrayals." Ed received his second Emmy nomination (Best Actor, Single Performance, Lead or Support) for his performance.

He also continued his string of guest appearances on lighter variety programs, such as Steve Allen and Perry Como. In February of 1958, Dinah Shore invited Ed to be a guest on her program, nearly a decade after her television debut on his variety show.

He reappeared on the big screen in April, in a small role as Uncle Samson in *Marjorie Morningstar.*

That same month, director George Stevens cast Ed in the film production of *The Diary of Anne Frank*, based on the world famous chronicle the thirteen-year-old girl kept as she, her family, and other Jews hid from the Nazis in an Amsterdam attic apartment. After the war, Anne's father Otto, the only member of his family to survive the concentration camps, retrieved the diary. Its publication and stage play adaptation followed. Ed was paid $50,000 for his work in the film.

He was cast as Albert Dussell, a single, middle-aged dentist the Frank family somewhat reluctantly takes in during their nearly two-year ordeal. As Dussell, Ed's first scene in the film is perhaps his most powerful. Upon his arrival at the family's attic hideout, he explains in a quiet, melancholy voice that many of the Frank's friends have already been shipped off to the camps. "They're gone," he concludes.

Dussell, sharing a cramped room with Anne (played by seventeen-year-old newcomer Millie Perkins), initially claims to get along fine with children. But as he becomes more settled in, he feels freer to express his gripes about some of the other occupants, including Anne herself, and her screams in her sleep due to horrific night terrors.

Ed, as Albert Dussell, shares his latest information and experiences as Anne (Millie Perkins) looks on.

Dussell's character was based on the real life Fritz Pfeffer, a dentist and orthodox Jew with whom Anne did not get along throughout their confinement together. A controversy arose in later years when Pfeffer's widow Charlotte, and son Werner, objected to how Anne's descriptions of him were exaggerated in both the play and film, thus damaging Pfeffer's memory. In addition, the dramatic adaptations portrayed Fritz/Dussell as being virtually ignorant of all Jewish traditions and holidays. A scene depicting the Frank family's Hanukka celebration has Dussell appearing totally unaware of the holiday's very existence. Frances Goodrich and Albert Hackett, the writers of both the play and screenplay, explained to the Pfeffers that the drama needed a character to be ignorant of Jewish traditions as a device to educate a non-Jewish movie audience (Goodrich and Hackett won the Pulitzer Prize for the stage drama).

Given the role he was assigned, however, Ed succeeded in expressing a spectrum of emotions—dejection, annoyance, fear, anger—and held his own among his more experienced co-stars, among them

Shelly Winters, Lou Jacobi, and Joseph Schildkraut.

In an interview for this book, Millie Perkins recalled working with Ed on the set.

> "I didn't know very much about him before he came on the show...I knew a little bit about who he was, and I loved him. The show was a very heavy emotional experience. For six months, we were locked in those rooms and worked hard dealing with that difficult situation, the history of the story. When Ed came on, in the middle of the shooting, he was amazing. He was a breath of fresh air and sunshine.
>
> "Everyone was so delighted to have him, especially George Stevens, who just loved him so much. I got to love Ed immediately, and he was just adorable to me. And I think he appreciated me a great deal, too. There was just something in Ed Wynn that was so dear and sweet and kind. He didn't make jokes, he didn't act a certain way that cheered everybody up, there was just something in him, when he walked on the set. He never tried to do anything to entertain us or please us. He just was Ed Wynn, and Ed Wynn was a delightful, dear human being. He was one of my good memories of that movie."

The irony that Ed Wynn the *actor* had become more sought after than Ed Wynn the *clown* did not go unnoticed by at least one of his friends, George Burns. "I think that even with all the success he had as a dramatic actor," Burns once wrote, "Ed missed making laughter. There just isn't any other sound in the world like the sound of an audience laughter...there's nothing that compares to it. I remember once I was in a meeting with Ed, we were talking about the show he was going to do for me, and suddenly he said, 'You know, George, there's something radically wrong when they hire me to make people cry and Perry Como to make people laugh'.

Ed in the 1959 *Twilight Zone* episode "One for the Angels."

Chapter 13: Better With Age

> *"Ed Wynn is nothing if not likeable. His whole fantastic comeback has come about without the midwifing of any publicity man, any public relations campaign. He has had the kind of publicity that money can't buy."*
> —*Pageant* magazine, 1957

Ed's newly rising star prompted him to try a regular TV series again. It had been eight years since he last hosted *All-Star Revue*. In early 1958, he filmed a sitcom pilot, *Stage Father*, about a retired vaudevillian and his son, a struggling stage actor. When the network passed on it, he tried another pilot, a comedy/drama called *My Old Man*. It was initially reported that "Wynn will appear as a grandfather involved in the adventures of his children and grandchildren." The concept was tweaked considerably before production began, and renamed *The Ed Wynn Show*, to air Thursday nights on NBC.

This new venture brought a rather homogenized comedy with it, with Ed portraying a kindly widower, caring for his two granddaughters upon the death of their parents.

Time magazine assessed the program as lightweight fare, sweet but lacking in real laughs:

> "*The Ed Wynn Show* covers much of the same ground [as *The Donna Reed Show* and *Father Knows Best*] with the same sentimental tarpaulin. Old Vaudevillian Wynn, who last year at 70 rose up as a dramatic actor in *The Great Man*, brings only hints of his legendary Palace clowning to his new

home—a simple frame house in a small college town. As a kindly widower raising two granddaughters—and all sorts of sagacious Cain with the town fathers—Wynn emits enough warmth to heat Buffalo for a month. It is as comedy that the show is not so hot."

An equally tepid response by viewers resulted in the show lasting only half a season. The last telecast aired on New Year's Day, 1959. But the early failure of the show did not discourage producers and casting directors from continuing to seek him out. In fact, 1959 would prove to be one of Ed's busiest and most successful years ever.

He kicked off the year by hosting an edition of *Kraft Music Hall* in January. In March, he signed a deal with Riverside Records to record the "Grandpa Magic" series of six kiddie records, written and produced by Leo Israel, one of the top children's record producers in the industry.

With the release of *The Diary of Anne Frank* on March 18, reviews were all over the map with their assessments of the film. The *New York Times*' Bosley Crowther wrote, "real magnificence glows in [Stevens'] picture," but frowned upon Millie Perkins' performance in the title role, asserting that she "does not rise to his level of spiritual splendor in the role of Anne."

Variety had a different gripe, reporting that the three-hour film "with all its technical perfection, the inspired direction and the sensitivity with which many of the scenes are handled, *Diary* is simply too long…Unlike the play, the picture leaves too little to the imagination." But Perkins was praised for her "charming and captivating performance."

As for Ed, *Variety* added, "Wynn registers solidly, and he tosses off his many good lines with style." The New York *Herald Tribune* also declared that "Ed Wynn is superb."

It all culminated with Ed's Academy Award nomination, for Best Supporting Actor in a drama.

With so many offers still coming his way, he discovered he didn't need to sacrifice his comedy entirely for his new career as a character actor. Over the next several years, he alternated between straight dramatic and light comedic roles on both TV and in films. This allowed him the chance to give his familiar comic persona a makeover of sorts, with a subtler touch. Ed Wynn the light comedy actor emerged as a toned-down version of the Perfect Fool he had created onstage almost forty years before. He became the lovable old eccentric, and, as such, made the most of each guest role he took on. His giggly delivery and *joie vivre* were very much in evidence in a number of his supporting appearances.

In April of 1959, Ed took a featured role in another television remake of a film classic. Audiences saw him in the role of Grandpa for a new version of *Meet Me in St. Louis*, with Jane Powell and Tab Hunter.

He had still more jobs to keep him busy for the remainder of the year. In the fall, Rod Serling invited him to star in an episode of Serling's new TV anthology series, *The Twilight Zone*. Serling's earlier skepticism of Ed's acting ability had been put to rest upon the airing of *Requiem for a Heavyweight*. So, the prolific writer took one of his older scripts, called "One For The Angels" (which had already aired on two earlier, pre-*Twilight Zone* programs), and rewrote it specifically for Ed.

Ed played the lead role of Lew Bookman, a small-time sidewalk salesman of various novelties and curious items of dubious value. It was only the sixth episode of *The Twilight Zone* to air, and has become one of Ed's best known television roles, thanks to *The Twilight Zone*'s long afterlife in syndication.

In the story, Mr. Death (Murray Hamilton) visits Bookman one fine day to inform him that he is scheduled to die at midnight. But Bookman asks for one favor first: that he not be taken until he makes one big sales pitch, "one for the angels," to satisfactorily cap off his career, and his life. Mr. Death agrees, but Bookman secretly intends to keep him waiting for that pitch for many years to come. When a little girl in Bookman's apartment building is hit by a car, Mr. Death then sets his sights on *her* for a midnight departure to Heaven. But he must not be late. Appalled by the prospect, Bookman intercepts Mr. Death's late-night arrival to take the girl, by delivering a long, compelling sales pitch to keep his soft-spoken adversary at bay until after the midnight deadline. The girl's condition then begins to improve, but since Bookman has just made the Big Pitch of his life, he honors the deal he made earlier, and quietly accompanies Mr. Death into the night.

The only problem with casting Ed in the role was that Bookman was meant to deliver a fast-talking spiel to his customers. Ed was wary of both the number of words and the speed at which he was supposed to deliver them. But Serling remained confident in his star (just as Martin Manulus had stubbornly stood by him during the *Requiem* rehearsals, in the face of Serling's objections). In the end, Ed's own familiar and endearing idiosyncrasies of speech more than made up for his lack of a rapid-fire technique.

For his next job, he accepted an offer from one particularly maligned comic genius named Jerry Lewis to join him in a new film, *Cinderfella*. Filming lasted two months, beginning on October 19.

Lewis, four years after his split from Dean Martin, was already becoming the unofficial whipping boy of American film critics. More often than not, they viewed his over-the-top antics onscreen as juvenile and self-indulgent, and saw Lewis—who was co-writing and directing his films—as being unable or unwilling to reign himself in, milking even mildly amusing gags way beyond their worth.

But history shows us that it was Lewis who almost single-handedly brought true slapstick comedy back to American films after the comatose decade of the 1950s. His films of the early '60s, such as *The Bellboy* and *The Errand Boy*, may have lacked anything resembling comic subtlety or restraint. But to his credit, and despite the grumbling from the critics, he kept throwing his gawky screen persona and preposterous sight gags straight at his audiences' heads, without let-up. He provided what had been missing from films for so long: an anything-for-a-laugh philosophy favoring silly, often surreal sight gags and a plethora of pratfalls, designed to do nothing more than to keep filmgoers in stitches. As fashionable as it became to denigrate him and his comic style, Lewis can be credited with helping American film comedy crawl out of its doldrums, which, throughout the 1950s, was no laughing matter.

Cinderfella, whose title succinctly describes its plot—a modern day reworking of the Cinderella fairy tale—except with a young male lead, nasty stepbrothers, and a dapper fairy godfather (played by Ed), who appears occasionally to offer advice and encouragement.

Lewis biographer Shawn Levy notes that Lewis was not one to share valuable screen time with just any fellow comedian, and that

Ed was "the only important comedian ever to play a major part in one of Jerry's films." Ed's role as the fairy godfather also provided a break from his string of dramatic film roles of the previous few years.

Before 1959 was over, Ed also starred in another television remake of a film classic, *Miracle on 34th Street*, playing of course, Kris Kringle.

That same year also saw the publication of Keenan's book, *Ed Wynn's Son*, in which he writes of his rocky relationship with Ed. It has ever since been the only source of any length or detail to give the public a close-up look at the dysfunctional Wynn family (and thus has been consulted and quoted to considerable degree for this book). Considering how Ed himself steadfastly refused throughout his life to pen his autobiography, Keenan's version was as close a look into the Wynn's personal life as the public could get.

But *The New York Times* reviewer Murray Schumach was not impressed with Keenan's dour account of life as the son of a show business legend. "The crying-towel school of literature has found another exponent in Keenan Wynn," the review began. "He wants the world to know it was tough to be the son of his famous father, Ed, and that a good deal of the misery was his own fault." Schumach found himself far more interested in stories about Ed than in those about the author, concluding, "What we have is an account of a spoiled brat who took a long time to mature in an exciting background."

As Keenan himself noted on the pages of the book, he was, at the age of forty-three, just beginning to come to terms with his upbringing, and with his father's shortcomings as a parent. The emotional wounds were then only beginning to heal. Keenan's own blossoming career no doubt helped the process, and he began to express considerable pride in his father's newfound success as an actor. "My own feelings toward Dad had been changing," he wrote. "Here was no sudden, overnight transformation of resentment into love…But little by little I was seeing my father as a man and feeling my heart warm toward him."

On April 15, 1960, Westinghouse Desilu Playhouse presented *The Man in the Funny Suit*, written and directed by *Requiem*'s director, Ralph Nelson. The production's concept made for what could be considered one of the most unusual dramatic presentations in television history. The story of Ed's troubles throughout the rehearsals for *Requiem* had, by then, become something of a legend among Hollywood insiders, but the general public remained largely unaware of the story. In *The Man In The Funny Suit*, nearly all of those involved in the original *Requiem* broadcast—Ed, Keenan, Jack Palance, Ned Glass, even Rod Serling and Red Skelton—all played themselves in a re-creation of the very rehearsal process that caused so much consternation at the time.

Nelson received an Emmy nomination for directing *The Man in the Funny Suit*, and, in an almost surreal final touch, Ed was nominated for Best Actor in a Drama for playing himself. It was undoubtedly the only time in show business history in which an actor was nominated for his portrayal of his own true-to-life difficulties *as an actor* (the effect being much like holding two mirrors face to face).

The next six years continued to bring a full workload for Ed, and he reveled in it. Most of his acting jobs in this last period of his life were comedic in nature, with a few light dramatic turns as well (but nothing along the lines of his roles in *Requiem for a Heavyweight*, or *The Diary of Anne Frank*).

Cinderfella was released on December 16, 1960 and, predictably, the critics were not pleased. *The New York Times* review called it "dismal...even the kids will be bored stiff...Only Ed Wynn manages to make a slight personal dent in the proceedings." The show business magazine *Box Office* magazine presented its Blue Ribbon Award to Ed for his performance.

The following year, he appeared in the Disney film *The Absent Minded Professor*, starring Fred MacMurray. Ed played, not coincidentally, a fire chief. Keenan had a part in the film as well. As his feelings toward his father slowly continued to thaw, Keenan offered less resistance to sharing screen time with Ed. *The Absent Minded Professor* was released on March 16, 1961.

From there, Ed appeared in TV programs ranging from the western *Rawhide*, to *The Red Skelton Show*, on which he appeared twice that year.

Another role well-suited to his talents was that of the Toymaker in the elaborate Disney re-make of *Babes in Toyland*, starring

Annette Funicello, Ray Bolger, and Tommy Sands. The film capped off 1961 with its December release, but was a commercial failure. However, *Box Office* magazine bestowed another Blue Ribbon Award to Ed for his performance.

On January 31, 1962, the newly formed Parkinson's Foundation named Ed honorary president. Its new headquarters, to be built in New York, would bear his name "in honor of his many years of extreme dedication to charitable efforts."

The rest of 1962 was relatively quiet for him, although he did host an odd little documentary of sorts, called *The Sound of Laughter*. Dressed as a college professor standing by a blackboard, he gives a comedy lesson by introducing scenes from various comedy films from decades past, while adding a few bits of business of his own in between the clips.

Job offers continued to come his way in 1963. In January, he appeared in *Son of Flubber*, the sequel to *The Absent Minded Professor*, and later appeared in five episodes of *77 Sunset Strip*, as a character named Ferenstein. On November 11, he appeared as a guest on *The Tonight Show* with its new host, Johnny Carson.

In December, Ed returned to *The Twilight Zone* to star in the episode "Ninety Years Without Slumbering." The story was not written by Rod Serling, but by one of the show's most reliable writers, George Clayton Johnson (although Johnson's story was altered considerably by another writer, at the order of series producer William Froug).

In the episode, Ed plays Sam Forstman, a man of about 70 who has become convinced that a grandfather clock he has owned all his life is, in fact, keeping him alive. He firmly believes that the moment the clock stops, he will die. His concerned daughter and son-in-law send him to a psychiatrist, whose attempts to have Sam see reason get nowhere. The clock is then sold to a neighbor, but Sam is determined to keep an eye on it and wind it regularly, especially when the neighbor leaves home for a vacation. At one point, the clock does wind down and stops before Sam can wind it again. As he is about to die, we see his spirit leave his body, but Sam then gets into an argument with himself, suddenly rejecting his long-held belief that his life is tied to that of the clock. His spirit (or possibly a figment of his imagination) disappears, and Sam awakens with a new, bright outlook on life. "Ninety Years Without Slumbering" aired on December 20, 1963, and, while it isn't perhaps as memorable, or of the same overall quality as "One For The Angels," it does boast another warm, dignified performance by Ed.

The following year, he played his best-known film role, in one of Disney's most successful and popular live-action films, *Mary Poppins*. As Mary's Uncle Albert, his frequent and hearty laughing fits come with a side effect that causes him to float to the ceiling every time his giggles get the best of him. This prompts the song "I Love To Laugh", in which chimney sweep Bert (Dick van Dyke) and the children under Mary's care join Albert for a gravity-defying afternoon tea. Mary finally leaves with the children, leaving Van Dyke and Ed to continue trading several corny and very Wynn-esque jokes with each other (possibly contributed by Ed himself). As Van Dyke recalled in an interview marking the 45th anniversary of the film's release, "He was in his [late 70s] at the time, and not very well. He did all that 'I Love To Laugh' stuff hanging from the ceiling, and it was just so hard on him, but he was trouper. He was a sweet old guy. He had a palsy [Parkinson's disease]—his head would move from side to side, kind of involuntarily. But the minute they would say 'Action,' it would stop. And he'd do the scene, and the minute they said 'Cut,' it would start in again."

The film was released August 27. Among other words of praise for the film, *The New York Times* succinctly reported, "Ed Wynn is grand."

And still the offers for work kept coming, so much so that he had to turn down the majority of those he received. On September 26, he hosted the long-running *Hollywood Palace* variety series. At one point in the program, he introduced comedian Jack Carter, who came out dressed as Ed's Perfect Fool character. Later, in a gag acknowledging the changing times—Beatlemania in particular—Ed donned a Beatles wig to sing *I Want To Hold Your Hand*, resulting in his getting mobbed by a group of excited lady senior citizens. He and Edie Gorme also sang "Tea For Two" on his piano bicycle. He closed the show in his customary fashion, by going to bed in his nightshirt & cap.

Ed also appeared in a *Bonanza* episode, "Ponderosa Birdman," filmed in November of 1964, and aired February 7,1965. He played

Ed and Dick Van Dyke in *Mary Poppins*.

Professor Phineas T. Klump, an eccentric inventor with a contraption that, he promised, could enable a man to fly.

One of the most elaborate and heartfelt tributes to Ed took place on May 7, 1965 at the Hollywood chapter of the National Academy of Television Arts and Sciences. The Tribute dinner for him, part of the Ninth Annual Ball, was held at the Beverly Hilton Hotel. Nearly 1,000 guests attended. Milton Berle hosted the evening's festivities, accompanied by Les Brown and his Band of Renown.

The printed program for the evening offered a rundown of the songs, comedy sketches, and speeches scheduled:

CITATION FOR ED WRITTEN BY ROD SERLING

I   Mr. Wynn (sung by Rose Marie)

II   The Wynn Ding-a-ling (Rose Marie, Jack Carter, et. al.)

III	This Was the Wynn That Was (written by Hal Kanter) Bill Conrad, Jack Carter
IV	Gone With the Wynn (Hy Averback, Jack Carter)
V	The Fugitive (David Janssen, Gene Barry, Robert Vaughn, Howard Morris)
VI	Peyton Place (Imogene Coca, Dorothy Provine)
VII	Special Awards (Cesar Romero, Bill Dana) Written by Dana, Bill Persky, Sam Denoff
VIII	Serling, Stirling, Spelling, Sperling (Pat Boone, Edd Byrnes, Marvin Kaplan)
IX	Conference Call (Edward Andrews, Paul Lynde) written by Bill Dana
X	Let Me Entertain You (Eddie Fisher)
XI	Epilogue (Milton Berle)

Variety reported on the evening's festivities. "Even before Milton Berle had finished with his intro, the celebrants were on their feet and gave Wynn a rousing ovation that lasted a full minute. At the close of his acceptance they were up again and Wynn almost wept."

Ed recalled that he invented the cue card "for guys with weak eyes and bad memories." He also turned the spotlight on his collaborators for his 1949 variety show—Hal Kanter, Ralph Levy, and Seaman Jacobs. *Variety* also noted, "It was Berle's night, too. No Vegas strip crowd ever howled more at his monologue."

The Academy actually lost money on the night, charging $25.00 per couple, while the Hilton charged Academy $11.50 per head. And the band bill totaled $1,500.

On November 18, Ed again appeared on TV screens as host of an NBC special presenting Ringling Brothers' Barnum & Bailey Circus, taped in Seattle. He shared a bit of screen time with his three granddaughters—Hilda, Edwyna, and Emily.

By this time, his health had begun to fail him, but he continued lining up work. He made another appearance on Red Skelton's show, followed by a supporting role in Disney's comedy-fantasy, *The Gnome Mobile*. Ed performed his role as the leader of a group of forest gnomes with considerable energy and expressiveness, providing one of the film's highlights.

In March, he went to Washington, D.C. to participate in a gathering of the American Parkinson's Disease Association, where he performed several times over the two days, and returned home exhausted. "When he came home from that trip," Keenan reported, "he began to show the results of the cancer." An operation for a tumor in Ed's neck revealed the malignancy in his throat.

Ed spent the last three months of his life in his Wiltshire Boulevard apartment. But as much as he adored his grandchildren, he refused to see them. More accurately, he refused to have them see their grandfather in failing health. "His appearance had changed," Keenan said, "and he couldn't talk. He wanted them to remember him as the roly-poly funnyman."

At 7:45 a.m. on June 19, 1966, Ed succumbed to his illness. After a non-denominational funeral service at Forest Lawn cemetery, he was cremated. The inscription on his memorial stone reads "Dear God—Thanks." In his will written a month before, Ed left most of his estate to Keenan.

Red Skelton said of Ed's passing, "His death was the first time that Ed Wynn ever made anyone sad."

Epilogue

That November 9, 1966, on what would have been Ed's 80th birthday, The American Parkinson Disease Association held a dinner salute to Ed, transmitted via closed circuit between New York, Los Angeles, and Chicago. Guests included Red Skelton, Dinah Shore, Milton Berle, Dean Martin, Lucille Ball, Dick van Dyke, and Debbie Reynolds.

On September 24, 1967, the association held another star-studded dinner at the New York Hilton, for the purpose of presenting the first annual Ed Wynn Humanitarian Award. Performers included singers Steve Lawrence & Edie Gormet and comedian Buddy Hackett. The Humanitarian Award went to New York radio personality William B. Williams, stalwart of WNEW, the station that rose from the ashes of Ed's failed Amalgamated Network thirty-five years earlier. Proceeds for the dinner went to a fund to create the Ed Wynn Rehabilitation Center in New York.

A more traditional show-business honor for Ed can be found on Hollywood Boulevard's Walk of Fame, on which three separate stars bear in his name—one for radio, another for motion pictures, and a third for TV, but surprisingly, not for his stage career.

Ed once said, "It is my hope that when I die the public will be sorry over having lost a favorite fool." Judging from the half-century of accolades, respect, and unrestrained laughter he elicited from his audiences, critics, and peers, it's safe to say that Ed got his wish. With his passing, the public did indeed lose not only a favorite fool, but the Perfect Fool.

Notes

Introduction

"The Perfect Fool for more than a half century..." Eddie Cantor, *The Way I See It*, (Englewood Cliffs, NJ: Prentice-Hall, Inc., 1959), p. 109.

"Unlike as in most of the arts, greatness in comedy is not necessarily judged by its ability to transcend generations...." Steve Martin, Introduction to *The Most of S.J. Perelman* (New York: Random House, 2000).

"Ed Wynn was one of the greatest comedians and actors that ever lived." Donald O'Connor, *Willamette Week* 1979.

"Any century is lucky if it has a clown or two..." Norman Lear, "And I Said To Myself" blog, Huffington Post, Jan. 14, 2007.

Harold Lloyd quote: Introduction to *The Laugh Makers* by William Cahn (New York: G.P. Putnam's Sons, 1957).

"Seven basic jokes" *Reader's Digest*, Sept. 1951, p. 99.

Chapter One:

Neil Simon quote from *Rewrites*, (New York, Simon & Schuster, 1996), page 50.

"As a young boy...I had a great sense of the ridiculous..." Interview with Max Wilk, August 9, 1960, New York Public Library, American Jewish Committee Oral History Collection.

"I used to be the biggest attraction on that beach..." *The Great Comedians* by Larry Wilde, (Secaucus: Citadel Press, 1968) p.370.

"My whole family was manufacturers of ladies hats..." Ibid., p.372.

"I was not a singer..." Ibid., p.371.

"There is a crumbling newspaper clipping..." Keenan Wynn, *Ed Wynn's Son* by Keenan Wynn, as told to James Brough, (New York: Doubleday & Company 1959), p.25.

"The only original thing in the [Joe Welch] monologue..." Theatre program for *The Laugh Parade*, published by the New York Theatre Program Corporation, 1931-32.

"After nineteen weeks..." Wilde, *The Great Comedians*, p.372.

"Looking back from today..." Henny Youngman (with Neal Karlen) *Take My Life, Please!* (New York: William Morrow & Company, 1991), p. 61.

"We Marx Brothers never denied our Jewishness..." Groucho Marx, *The Groucho Phile* (Indianapolis/New York: Bobbs-Merrill, 1976),p.21

"When I first went on the stage..." Max Wilk interview.

"You could be ignorant and be a star..." Fred Allen, *Much Ado About Me*, (Boston: Little, Brown & Company, 1956) p.240.

Chapter Two

Harpo quote about vaudevillians: *Harpo Speaks* (New York, Freeway Press, 1974), p. 100.

"We revolutionized the two-man comedy act..." *Life* magazine, "August Clown" by Joel Sayre, July 26, 1948, p.65.

"We took five bows..." and "I've never felt better since I've been on the road..." from post cards written by Ed, sent home from his travels, are part of the Philadephia Free Library's Theatre Collection.

"I believe all comedians arrive by trial and error..." Groucho Marx, *Groucho And Me*, (New York: Manor Books Inc., 1959), p.87

"Mr. Wynn...is on the go during the rest of the piece..." N.Y. Mirror, November 7, 1908.

"Among the novelties..." Review, "Novelties Galore Shown at Keith's" *Philadephia Enquirer*, Jan. 5, 1909.

"With Ed Wynn and a company of 15..." *Syracuse Journal* January 25, 1909.

"Mr. Wynn proved as capably eccentric..." *NY Mirror* February 27, 1909.

"Ed Wynn, with Al Lee, is back in his own act..." *Variety*, June 12, 1909.

"An amusing pair..." *San Francisco Call*, 9/26/09

"I found that costumes were a part of it..." *The Great Comedians*, p.371

"There used to be a bar on 48th and Broadway..." *The New York Times Magazine*, "Ed Wynn: Up-and-Coming Actor," May 12, 1957, p. 28.

The Deacon and the Lady review, *The New York Times*, October. 5, 1910.

"Ed Wynn returns to vaudeville with a new partner, from the legitimate..." *Variety* magazine, Dec. 17, 1910.

Chapter Three

"Cantor never called him Flo." Ned Wynn quoting Ed, *We'll Always Live in Beverly Hills* (Penguin, 1992), p. 68.

"Keenan has raised 'Man to Man...'" *San Francisco Call*, June 23, 1912.

"They [vaudeville] used to announce acts..." Opening at Palace, *The New York Times Magazine*, May 12, 1957, p. 28

Lulu McConnell and Jester sketch suggestion: "August Clown" by Joel Sayre, *Life* magazine, July 26, 1948, p. 65.

"lucky undershirt" *The Evening Bulletin*, Philadelphia, "Being Funny Makes Ed Wynn Very Sad" April 4, 1932.

"I played a couple of instruments..." *The Great Comedians*, p. 371.

"You should see the motion picture rehearsal..." Ziegfeld *Follies* of 1915 review, The New York Times, June 22, 1915.

"In the early days of vaudeville..." Max Wilk interview.

"Fields was a tough guy." Groucho Marx, *Playboy* magazine. March 1974, p. 72.

The Passing Show of 1916 review, *The New York Times*, June 23, 1916.

Sometime review, *The New York Times*, October. 5, 1918.

Shubert Gaieties of 1919 review: *The New York Times*, by John Corbin, July 8. 1919.

"I have nothing to gain in this fight..." *N.Y. Telegram* Aug 12, 1919.

"At last I am proud of my Jewish son-in-law." Ibid.

Ruth Peiter, *The Toledo Times*, Jan. 20, 1920.

Carnival review *The New York Times*, April 6, 1920.

"Wynn's comedy in his *Carnival* show..." *The Toledo Blade*, "Will Ed Wynne's Nut Comedy Go on the Screen?" Nov. 24, 1920.

CHAPTER FOUR

"Personality is an amazing thing..." *Vanity Fair*, June 1920.

"I remember they had some Japanese costumes...other sets, other numbers." "Ed Wynn: Up-and-Coming Actor." *The New York Times*, May 12, '57 p. 30

The Perfect Fool review, *The New York Times* November 8, 1921.

Grab Bag review, *The New York Times*, Oct. 7, 1924.

White Rats, Actors Union worried about movies in vaudeville shows, *The New York Times*, Feb. 13, 1908.

"They rejected my titles, most of my story..." *Rubber Heels* review, *The New York Times*, June 28, 1927.

"He had modestly effaced himself..." *Manhattan Mary* review, *The New York Times*, September 27, 1927.

"...she could say the most dreadful things..." *Ed Wynn's Son*, p. 66

Chapter Five

"A person is not a success because of what he has to offer..." Ed quoted in *The New York Times*, October 7, 1934, sect. 8, p. 10.

"For every hickery-dickery dock..." *The New York Times*, Feb. 23, 1930 "Envoy For Mother Goose."

"With *Simple Simon*, I was the only actor-partner Ziegfeld ever had..." "Ed Wynn: Up-and-Coming Actor" *The New York Times Magazine* May 12, '57 p. 30

"...I found I was getting engaged to myself..." Ibid.

"It is Ed Wynn's field day..." Review of *Simple Simon* by Brooks Atkinson, *The New York Times*, February 19, 1930, p. 22.

Follow The Leader review by Mordaunt Hall, *The New York Times*, Dec. 6, 1930.

Follow The Leader review, Exhibitors Forum, Feb. 10, 1930.

"Ed Wynn is still the most winning and likable of the buffoons..." *The New York Times*, May 4, 1931.

"With a few loyal helpers..." *Radio Stars* magazine, "You Can't Keep Him Down!" by Curtis Mitchell, May, 1933.

Time magazine review of *The Laugh Parade*, November 16, 1931.

"Marshall of the Laugh Parade" by J. Brooks Atkinson, *The New York Times*, December 6, 1931.

"Ed Wynn, King of Idiocy" by John Mason Brown, *Two on the Aisle* (New York: W.W. Norton & Company) 1938, p. 270.

Chapter Six

"I guess the biggest adjustment we all had to make..." *All My Best Friends*, p. 134.

"If I had to do it all over again..." *Evening Bulletin* (Philadelphia), "Being Funny Makes Ed Wynn Very Sad," April 4, 1932.

"If his brand of humor..." *Ed Wynn's Son*, p.85.

"I would say that my father was a very gentle man..." Keenan in his introduction to the LP record "Ed Wynn The Fire Chief as the Perfect Fool", containing two of Ed's radio broadcasts. Produced by George Garabedian for Mark 56 Records, 1973.

"...radio was a medium where, every week, more people would hear my jokes..." *Don't Shoot, It's Only Me*, by Bob Hope with Melville Shavelson, p. 28.

"In the theatre, the actor had uncertainty..." *Treadmill to Oblivion*, p. 3.

"Keeping an audience under glass was one thing..." *All My Best Friends*, p. 133.

"The audience is howling..." Eddie Cantor, *The Way I See It*.

"A man with no talent..." Ed assesses Eddie Cantor, quoted by Ned Wynn, *We'll Always Live in Beverly Hills* by Ned Wynn, p. 68.

"[Cantor] wore funny costumes..." *Treadmill to Oblivion*, p. 4.

"Eddie Cantor had to fight for his laughs..." Milton Berle, *B.S. I Love You*.

"To sit by a radio receiver and hear laughter..." John Carlisle complains: *The New York Times*, July 24, 1932, section 9, p.1.

"That sort of stumped me." "This Business of Being Funny On Radio Is No Joke, Says Wynn" *The New York Times*, May 29, 1932.

"How can one man please twenty million people?." Ibid.

"In can't act funny unless I dress funny." *Liberty* magazine, "The Private Life of Ed Wynn by Clara Beranger, August 31, 1935.

Review of first Fire Chief broadcast, *Variety*, April 27, 1932.

"It would be an impossibility for any comedian to create..." "Playing For Laughs." By Richard O'Brien *The New York Times*, April 23, 1933, section 9, p.5.

"I have never worked so hard on any job..." *The New York Times*, May 29, 1932.

"When we all went into radio..." *All My Best Friends*, p. 134.

Ed speaks of *The Philosophy of a Fool, Harvard Crimson*, November 8, 1937.

"I've always been accustomed to cavort..." *The New York Times*, May 29, 1932.

"He was a clown..." Keenan's introduction to LP record of Ed's broadcasts.

"It seemed to me that the bizarre-garbed..." Fred Allen, *Treadmill to Oblivion*, p. 5.

"...approximately 200 possibilities are discarded..." O'Brien, *The New York Times*, "Playing For Laughs."

"There isn't a Tuesday that I'm not as nervous as a man who faces a death sentence." Ibid.

"In radio's golden age..." *Sunday Nights At Seven*, p. 141

Chapter Seven

"Wynn, the undefeated..." *Radio Stars* magazine, March 1935 "Broken-hearted, Yet He Laughs" by George Kent.

"I have no desire to be the richest man in the cemetery." *The Harvard Crimson*, November 8, 1937.

"I'm stunned by my own success..." "Soooooo! The Fire Chief Comes to Hollywood!" By Faith Service

The New York Times' review of *The Chief* film, December 2, 1933.

Ed believes film studios are trying to kill off radio: Max Wilk interview.

"I'm going to present a humorous slant on big news items..." *The New York Times*, "They Still Laugh After 30 Years," October 7, 1934, sect. 8, p. 10.

"To think that people can still laugh at me..." Ibid.

"I am the most unhappy man in the world..." "The Private Life of Ed Wynn" by Clara Beranger, *Liberty* magazine Aug.. 31, 1935.

"In all true comedy, there must be an undercurrent of pathos..." Ibid.

"How long can he go on giving the world..." George Kent, *Radio Stars* magazine.

"He was lonely in a special way." *Ed Wynn's Son*, p.103.

Chapter Eight

"There have been times in my life…" *Tune In* magazine, "Laughing For A Living" by Ed Wynn, January, 1945.

"Dramatic actors are all new to me…" *The New York Times*, "When There's A Wynn There's a Way," February 9, 1936.

Alice Takat review in *The New York Times*, February 11, 1936.

"I've already got more ideas…" *The New York Times*, February 9, 1936.

"I'd like to appoint myself a committee of one…*The New York Times*, Dec. 6, 1936. "A Jules Verne Comedian" section 12, p. 14.

Frieda at Miss America pageant, "judged most suitable in an evening dress": *Time* magazine, September 19, 1927.

"For years I've made up my own lines…" Philadelphia Bulletin, November, 1937 (exact date unknown).

Hooray For What! review, Atkinson, *The New York Times*, December 2, 1937.

"Ed Wynn, for all his preposterous costumes…" *Hooray For What!* review, *Stage* magazine, January, 1938, p.8.

"After their curtain call…" *The Other Side of Ethel Mertz* by Frank Castelluccio and Alvin Walker, p.106.

"I received a salary of thirty-five dollars a week…" Dorothy Bird, *Bird's Eye View* by Dorothy Bird and Joyce Greenberg (Pittsburgh: University of Pittsburgh Press, 1997.), p. 146.

Frieda calls him "constant nag" at home. Associated Press (as reported in *The New York Times*) March 30, 1939.

"Though his stock in trade is the oldest..." *Boys and Girls Together!* review, *Theatre Arts* magazine, November 1940, p.773.

Boys and Girls Together review by Brooks Atkinson, *The New York Times*, October 13, 1940, section 9, p.1.

"It is no business of a drama reviewer to comment on an actor's personal calamities..." Atkinson, *The New York Times*, Oct. 18, 1940.

Boys and Girls Together review by Joseph Wood Krutch, *The Nation*, Oct. 12, 1940.

"Friday night I saw the Ed Wynn show..." Groucho letter to Irving Brecher, Dec. 16, 1940, *The Groucho Letters* (New York: Doubleday, 1967), reprinted Manor Books, Inc. 1974.

Laugh, Town, Laugh review, *The New York Times*, June 23, 1942.

Laugh, Town, Laugh review, *Time* magazine, July 6, 1942.

Laugh, Town, Laugh review, *Billboard*, July 4, 1942.

"There aren't enough headliners..." *Billboard*, May 9, 1942.

"Dressed in his weirdest hand-me-downs..." *Big Time* review, *Billboard*, March 13, 1943.

"This boy was all my audiences rolled up into one..." *Tune In* magazine, "Laughing For A Living" by Ed Wynn, January, 1945.

CHAPTER NINE

"Ed Wynn started a night club engagement the other day..." *The New York Times* magazine, February 1, 1948, p. 12.

Happy Island premieres, *The New York Times*, Sept. 17, 1944.

Happy Island review, *Time* magazine, September 25, 1944.

Happy Island review, *Billboard*, Oct. 14, 1944.

Ed calls TV "a thing more dangerous than dynamite..." *The New York Times*, December 13, 1944, p. 25.

"Laughing For A Living" by Ed Wynn, *Tune In* magazine, January, 1945.

Changes on Happy Island: *Billboard*, January 13, 1945.

"If any nitery in town can make a buck..." *Billboard*, January 17, 1948

"the applause could literally be heard outside." Ibid.

Review of "Scudda Hay" at Roxy: *Billboard*, April 24, 1948.

Ed offered to replace Frank Fay in *Harvey*: "August Clown" by Joel Sayre, *Life* magazine. July 26, 1948, p. 65.

"It proved once more, that television has a long way to go..." review of Edgar Bergen on TV. *Newsweek*, November 25, 1946.

CHAPTER TEN

"It was murder..." *The Great Comedians*, p.74.

"With television, no one will particularly wish to see..." Lewis Nichols, "Lament for the Age of Clowns, *The New York Times Magazine*, February 1, 1948, p. 12.

Laugh Carnival review by Edward Murphy, *Billboard*, November 20, 1948.

"Marriage with the public that will never be annulled": *Newsweek*, October 3, 1949.

"We're going to bust TV wide open." *Time* magazine review, October 17, 1949.

"I've yet to see something original from that man." Ibid.

All quotes by Hal Kanter, Martin Manulis, Barney McNulty, and Seaman Jacobs: All worked with Ed on his first TV show in 1949 and/or other programs. All were interviewed separately on video for the Archive of American Television (created by the Academy of Television Arts & Sciences. Hal Kanter was interviewed on May 22, 1997; Martin Manulis, June 17, 1997; Barney McNulty, December 9, 1997; Seaman Jacobs, March 30, 1999.

The New York Times review of *The Ed Wynn Show*, October 16, 1949.

"If Wynn's shenanigans..." *Life* magazine, October 17, 1949, p. 75.

"I'm still figuring out how much I can talk..." *The New York Times Magazine*, "Ed Wynn Conquers His Fourth Medium," October 23, 1948, p. 21.

"They had been looking forward to throwing the custard pies..." Buster Keaton, *My Wonderful World of Slapstick*, p. 256.

"You saved the show for me tonight." Ibid, p. 257.

"I think the episodes are excellent." Max Wilk interview.

The New York Times review of *Four Star Revue* (with guest Edith Piaf), October 5, 1950.

"So far results have not been spectacular..." *Life* magazine, Oct. 23, 1950.

George Burns: "[Television] wasn't like vaudeville…" George Burns, *All My Best Friends*, p. 276.

"The old-timers had audience acceptance in advance…" *Look* magazine, April 10, 1951.

Gracie memorizing lines: "Just a Couple of Performers," *The New York Times*, October 22, 1950, sec. 2, p. 13.

Fred Allen to Groucho Marx: "You are fortunate, I think…" letter dated Oct. 13, 1950 *The Groucho Letters*.

Fred Allen to Groucho Marx: "The revue type of show is the wrong approach…" Ibid.

Chapter Eleven

"At the top of his early success he martyred himself…" *Ed Wynn's Son*, p. 194.

Alice In Wonderland review: Bosley Crowther, *The New York Times*, July 30, 1951, p.12.

"What one remembers specifically about the tea party…" Leonard Maltin, *The Disney Films* (New York: Hyperion, 1984).

Keenan says Ed felt embarrassed on *This Is Your Life*. *Life* magazine, June 17, 1957.

Pilot for TV show with Rube Goldberg: *Billboard*, September 26, 1953.

"If a man has been an office worker all his life…" *Pageant* magazine October, 1957, p. 123.

"Durable, lovable Ed Wynn headlines the Ramona Room…" *Billboard*, November 20, 1954.

"I went up to see his show on his 68th birthday…" *Life* magazine, "A Warm Father" June 17, 1957.

Dorothy's reasons for divorcing Ed: *The New York Times*, March 1, 1955.

"When I wasn't working, I'd get a little ache..." *Life* magazine, June 17, 1957.

"After 53 years, I couldn't get any work..." *Pageant* magazine, October , 1957.

CHAPTER TWELVE

"It's just remarkable..." *Pageant* magazine, October, 1957, p. 120.

"I was scared as a kid..." Ibid, p. 121.

"Ed Wynn is outstanding..." *Variety* review of *The Great Man* January 1, 1956.

"The first thing I had to do was unlearn..." *Requiem* review: *The New York Times*, October 7, 1956.

"We had to devise tricks..." *Life* magazine, "A Warm Father," June 17, 1957.

"As soon as the show ended, everybody rushed over to me..." *Pageant* magazine, "Everybody's Happy For Ed," by Edward Linn, October 1957, p. 122

"Here I am, Ed Wynn's son again." *Life* magazine, June 17, 1957.

CHAPTER THIRTEEN

"Considering the pallid comedy..." Bosley Crowther, *The New York Times*, April 3, 1960, sect. 2, p.1

"For his last ten years..." Keenan intro to LP record.

Anonymous comedy writers: *The New York Times*, June 24, 1956.

"Good laughs—rich, full-bellied yoks and boffs..." *Life* magazine, April, 1957.

"I had violated one of my basic rules of work..." *Milton Berle: An Autobiography*, p.318

"The theme was so close to me..." *Pageant* magazine, Oct. 1957, p. 123

"This transition has caused quite a mental upheaval..." *The New York Times* magazine, "Ed Wynn: Up-and-Coming Actor." May 12. 1957, p. 14.

"There's a place in the story..." Ibid.

"Occasionally I mused over the possibility of making a sound film." Chaplin

"There is hardly a comedian alive who isn't capable of..." *Groucho and Me*, p.89.

"The hard job is doing comedy..." *The Great Comedians*, p. 318.

"As the Perfect Fool, I wasn't a real persona at all..." *Pageant* magazine, p.122.

"As a dramatic actor, you have to sit down and communicate..." Ibid.

"Ed Wynn Making Comeback on TV" *The New York Times*, Feb. 22, 1957.

Command Appearance broadcast: "a warm, bubbly, graceful tribute..." *Billboard*, September 20, 1957.

"What a pity the producers..." *The New York Times*, Sept. 20, 1957, p. 51.

"Mr. Wynn added to his roster of expert character portrayals." Jack Gould, *The New York Times*, November 18, 1957.

Millie Perkins interview with the author in 2010.

Ed to George Burns: "Something wrong when they hire me to make people cry...": *All My Best Friends*, p. 295.

Chapter Fourteen

"Ed Wynn is nothing if not likeable." *Pageant* magazine, p. 123.

Ed Wynn Show (sitcom) review, *Time* magazine, Oct. 13, 1958.

The Diary of Anne Frank review by Bosley Crowther, *The New York Times*, March 19, 1959.

Murray Schumach's review of *Ed Wynn's Son* in *The New York Times*, October 11, 1959.

"My own feelings toward Dad had been changing..." *Ed Wynn's Son*, p. 203.

Dick Van Dyke on "Mary Poppins" *Larry King Live*, CNN, March 19, 2009.

Television Academy dinner for Ed: *Variety*, May 19, 1965.

"When he came home from that trip..." Bob Thomas, The Associated Press (as printed in *The New York Times*), June 20, 1966.

Red Skelton: "His passing was the first time Ed Wynn made anyone sad." *Time* magazine, July 1, 1966 p.37.

Epilogue

"It is my hope that when I die..." *Everybody's Magazine*, August, 1925, p. 154.

BIBLIOGRAPHY

Allen, Fred. *Much Ado About Me*. Boston: Little, Brown & Company, 1956.

Allen, Fred. *Treadmill to Oblivion*. Boston: Little, Brown & Company, 1954.

Benny, Jack and Joan Benny. *Sunday Nights at Seven*. New York: Warner Books, 1990.

Berle, Milton with Haskel Frankel. *Milton Berle—An Autobiography*. New York: Delacorte Press, 1974.

Berle, Milton. *B.S. I Love You*. New York, McGraw-Hill, 1988.

Bird, Dorothy, and Joyce Greenberg. *Bird's Eye View*. Pittsburg: University of Pittsburgh Press, 1997.

Brooks, Tim and Earl Marsh. *The Complete Directory to Prime Time Network and Cable TV Shows* (Sixth Edition). NewYork: Ballantine Books, 1995.

Burns, George with David Fisher. *All My Best Friends*. New York: G.P. Putnam's Sons, 1989.

Cantor, Eddie. *The Way I See It*. Englewood Cliffs, N.J.: Prentice-Hall, Inc. 1959.

Castelluccio, Frank, and Alvin Walker. *The Other Side of Ethel Mertz*. Berkley, 2000.

Chaplin, Charles. *My Autobiography*. Random House UK, 1964.

Dunning, Johm. *On The Air: The Encyclopedia of Old-Time Radio*. New York, NY: Oxford University Press, 1998.

Fields, Ronald J. (editor) *W.C. Fields by Himself*. Englewood Cliffs, N.J. : Prentice-Hall, Inc. 1973.

Hope, Bob with Melville Shavelson. *Don't Shoot, It's Only Me*. New York: G.P. Putnam's Sons. 1990.

Keaton, Buster, and Charles Samuels. *My Wonderful World of Slapstick*. New York: Da Capo Press, 1960.

Leider, Emily Wortis. *Becoming Mae West*.

Levi, Shawn. *King of Comedy: The Life and Art of Jerry Lewis*. New York: St. Martin's Griffin, 1996.

Marx, Groucho. *Groucho and Me*. New York: Bernard Geis Associates, 1959.

Marx, Groucho. *The Groucho Letters*. New York: Manor Books, 1967.

Marx, Groucho and Richard J. Anobile. *The Marx Brothers Scrapbook*. New York: Grosset & Dunlap, 1974.

Marx, Harpo, with Rowland Barber. *Harpo Speaks*. New York: Freeway Press, 1974.

Parish, James Robert and William T. Leonard. *The Funsters*. New Rochelle, N.Y.: Arlington House, 1979.

Miriam Spitzer. *The Palace*. New York: Atheneum, 1969.

Stein, Charles (editor). *American Vaudeville—As Seen by its Contemporaries*. New York: Alfred A. Knopf, 1984.

Wilde, Larry. *The Great Comedians*. Secaucus, N.J.: Citadel Press, 1968.

Wynn, Keenan and James Brough. *Ed Wynn's Son.* Garden City, NY: Doubleday & Company, Inc. 1959.

Wynn, Ned. *We'll Always Live In Beverly Hills*. New York: William Morrow & Company, Inc. 1990.

Zicree, Scott Mark. *The Twilight Zone Companion*. New York: Bantam Books, 1982.

INDEX

Abbott & Costello, 109, 161, 163
Absent-minded Professor, The, 178
Ackerman, Harry, 150
Actor's Equity (strike), 41
Albee, Edward, 13
Alcoa Hour, 166
Alice in Wonderland, 147
Alice Takat, 95-96
All-Star Revue (see also: *Four-Star Revue*), 148,
163, 173
Allen, Fred, 17, 71, 73-75, 81, 83, 90-91, 97,
110, 123-124, 138, 141,144
Allen, Steve, 151
Amalgamated Broadcasting System, 87, 91-92
Amos & Andy, 142
Anderson, Eddie "Rochester", 130, 144-145
Arbuckle, Roscoe, 130
Arden, Eve, 130
Arlen, Harold, 98
Arnaz, Desi, 132
Arnold, Edward, 148
Astaire, Fred and Adele, 39
Atkinson, J. Brooks, 4, 61, 102, 108

Atoll K, 161

Babes In Toyland, 178
Ball, Lucille, 6, 132, 185
Bankhead, Tallulah, 110
Beck, Martin, 15
Bellboy, The, 176
Benny, Jack, 4, 16, 71, 86, 90-91, 123-124,
128, 143, 159, 167
Bergen, Edgar, 110, 123
Berle, Milton, 74, 86, 124-129, 134, 163, 165, 181
Berman, Shelley, 165
Big Broadcast films, 91
Big Time, 112
Billboard magazine, 111-112, 116, 122, 127,
128, 134, 168
Billiken Freshman, 23
Bird, Dorothy, 104
Blair, Janice, 168
Blair, Nicky, 120
Blanc, Mel, 144
Blue, Ben, 130
Bob & Ray, 123
Bolger, Ray, 110, 178

Bolton, Guy, 60
Bonanza, 180
Borge, Victor, 148
Born Yesterday, 161
Box Office magazine, 178
Boys and Girls Together, 106
Brecher, Irving, 109
Brice, Fanny, 32, 46, 95, 142
Brown, Joe E., 130
Brown, John Mason, 67
Brown, Les, 181
Bruce, Lenny, 165
Buck, Gene, 32-33
Buck Privates, 109
Burns, George, 16, 30, 69, 72, 75, 81, 141, 171
Burns & Allen, 91, 128, 143, 149

Caesar, Sid, 163
Caesar's Hour, 159, 163
Camp Shows, Inc., 113
Cantor, Eddie, 4, 72-74, 83, 86, 97, 110, 123, 138
Carlisle, John, 74
Carrot Top, 7
Carson, Jack, 137
Carson, Johnny, 179
Cerf, Bennett, 151
Century Midnight Whirl, 40
Chaplin, Charlie, 3, 27, 95, 160-161, 166-167
Chase, Charley, 90
Christians, Mady, 95
Cinderfella, 176-178
City Lights, 167
Clark, Bobby, 138, 141, 145
Cobb, Irvin S., 22
Cobert, Claudette, 161
Colgate Comedy Hour, The, 138, 145, 149, 163

Colonna, Jerry, 147
Como, Perry, 171
Conklin, Chester, 54
Court Jester, The, 30
Crouse, Russell, 98
Crowther, Bosley, 147, 162, 174

Dance With Me, Henry, 163
Davis, Bette, 110
Day, Dennis, 144
Day, Doris, 161
Deacon and the Lady, The, 25
DeHaven, Gloria, 130
DeRita, Joe, 161
Diary of Anne Frank, The, 169-171, 174
Doing Our Bit, 39
Donna Reed Show, The, 173
Durante, Jimmy, 110, 137, 148-149

Ebsen, Buddy, 130
Edwards, Ralph, 150
Ed Sullivan Show, The, 150
Ed Wynn's Carnival, 45
Ed Wynn Show, The (1949), 129-
Ed Wynn Show, The (1958), 173-174
Ed Wynn's Son, 177
Ellison, Jack, 129
Erlinger, E.L., 25
Errand Boy, The, 176
Erroll, Leon, 32-33, 46, 130

Fay, Frank, 122
Father Knows Best, 173
Ferrer, Jose, 153-154
Fibber McGee & Molly, 118-119
Fields, Lew, 13
Fields, W.C., 3, 23, 27, 34-35, 41, 46, 48, 75, 90, 106, 160
Finklehoffe, Fred, 112

Fire Chief, The (radio program), 4, 77-81, 83-84, 87, 94, 120
Flick, Pat, 106
Follow The Leader, 62
Four-Star Revue, 137-141
Francis, Arlene, 151
Freed, Arthur, 106
Frings, Kurt, 153
Funicello, Annette, 178

Gallagher, 7
Garbo, Greta, 95
Gobel, George, 153
George Gobel Show, 151
George White's Scandals, 46
Glass, Ned, 156-157, 178
Gleason, Jackie, 6, 163
Gnombe-Mobile, The, 183
Godfrey, Arthur, 141
Goldberg, Rube, 150
Goodrich, Frances, 170
Gorme, Edie, 180, 185
Gould, Jack, 116, 129
Grant, Cary, 161
Grab Bag, The, 50-51
Grandpa Magic records, 174
Great American Hoax, The, 166
Great Man, The, 153-154
Greenberg, Samuel and Ruth, 58, 92-93
Gulliver the Traveler, 97

Hackett, Albert, 170
Hackett, Buddy, 185
Haley, Jack, 110
Hall, Mordant, 62
Hallmark Television Playhouse, 169
Hamilton, Margaret, 169
Hamilton, Murray, 175
Hammerstein, Arthur, 39

Happy Island, 115-117, 119
Harburg, E.Y., 98, 106
Harlow, Jean, 95
Hart, Lorenz, 61
Harvey, 122
Haymes, Dick, 130
Hellman, Jack, 131
Herald Tribune, 174
Herman, Pee Wee, 7
Holliday, Judy, 161
Hollywood Palace, The, 180
Hooray For What!, 98-104
Hope, Bob, 70, 123, 148, 159
Horn Blows at Midnight, The, 91
Howard, Shemp, 161
Hudson, Rock, 161
Hunter, Tab, 175

I Love Lucy, 6, 102, 132, 134, 149
I Married Joan, 149
I Remember Mama, 95
International House, 75, 91
In The Navy, 109
Israel, Leo, 174
It's In The Bag, 91

Jackie Gleason Show, The, 149
Jacobi, Lou, 171
Jacobs, Seaman, 128, 129, 182
Jennings, P. O'Malley, 26
Jessel, George, 86
Jordan, Jim & Marion, 118

KDKA, 48
Kalmar, Bert, 88
Kanter, Hal, 130, 182
Karloff, Boris, 110
Karno, Fred, 26
Kaye, Danny, 110
Keaton, Buster, 3, 130, 136-137
Kelly, Gene, 113

Keep 'Em Flying, 109
Keith, Benjamin Franklin, 14
Kelly, Harry, 25
Keenan, Frank, 29-30, 41
Kennan (Wynn), Hilda, 29-30, 34, 36-38, 50-53, 55-58, 69, 92, 98, 106
Kent, George, 93
Keystone Kops, 136
Kilgallen, Dorothy, 151
King in New York, A, 161
Kovacs, Ernie, 163
Kraft Music Hall, 174
Krutch, Joseph Wood, 108

Lahr, Bert, 86, 112
Laugh Carnival, 127
Laugh Parade, The, 63-67, 69, 76, 81-82, 95
Laughton, Charles, 130
Laugh, Town, Laugh!, 110-111
Laurel & Hardy, 90, 150, 160-161
Laurel, Stan, 27
Lawrence, Steve, 185
Lear, Norman, 6
Lee, Al, 23
Lemmon, Jack, 161
Leopold, Joseph, 10, 12, 17, 50
Leopold, Leon, 10, 123
Leopold, Minnie, 10, 17, 50
LeRoy, Mervyn, 106
Levy, Ralph, 182
Levy, Shawn, 176
Lewis, Jack, 20, 23
Lewis, Jerry, 5, 168, 176
Lewis, Joe E., 112
Life magazine, 57, 141, 163
Llly, Beatrice, 168
Limelight, 161
Lindsay, Howard, 98
Lloyd, Harold, 7, 55

Lombard, Carole, 161, 167
Look magazine, 143
Louis, Joe, 110

Mack, Ted, 127
MacMurray, Fred, 178
Manager's Protective Association, 42, 45
Manhattan Mary, 55
Man in the Funny Suit, The, 177
Manulus, Martin, 155-157
Marjorie Morningstar, 169
Martin & Lewis, 138, 162-163
Martin, Dean, 185
Marx Brothers, 3, 54, 90, 122, 160
Marx, Chico, 27
Marx, Groucho, 5, 16, 21, 27, 35, 86, 109, 128, 145, 168
Marx, Harpo, 19
Mary Poppins, 180
Meet Me In St. Louis, 175
McConnell, Lulu, 31
McCullough, Paul, 145
McNamee, Graham, 77-79, 82
McNulty, Barney, 131-132
Merman, Ethel, 62
Mierse (Wynn), Frieda, 98, 104-105
Minnelli, Vincente, 101
Miranda, Carmen, 130
Miracle on 34th Street, 177
Modern Times, 95
Moore, Victor, 130
Mr. Busybody, 22
My Man Godfrey, 167

Navy Relief Society (benefit show), 109
Neilsen, Gertrude, 129
Nelson, Ralph, 155-157
Nesbitt (Wynn), Dorothy, 109, 127, 136, 152

Newhart, Bob, 165
New Look Revue, The, 120-122
New York Times, The, 25, 36, 40, 45, 48, 55, 57, 63, 95, 111, 115, 127, 129, 140, 147, 162, 168-169, 174, 177, 178
Nichols, Lewis, 127
Nichols & May, 165
Nothing Sacred, 167

Oberon, Merle, 110
O'Brien, Virginia, 130
O'Connor, Donald, 6
Olsen & Johnson, 110, 148
On Borrowed Time, 169
Operation Petticoat, 161
Orpheum Circuit, 15
Our Gang (The Little Rascals), 90
Our Miss Brooks, 149
Over the Top, 39

Pageant magazine, 173
Palace Theatre, 30-31
Palance, Jack, 155, 178
Parkinson's Foundation, 179
Passing Show of 1916, 36
Pearl, Jack, 83, 90-91
Pemberton, Brock, 122
Perfect Fool, The, 46-48
Perkins, Millie, 169-171, 174
Pfeiffer, Fritz, 170
Philadelphia Inquirer, 22
Philosophy of a Fool, The, 82
Piaf, Edith, 139-141
Pickens, Jane, 120
Pickford, Mary, 75
Pillow Talk, 161
Playhouse 90, 154
Please Don't Eat The Daisies, 162
Porter, Cole, 60

Powell, Jane, 175
Powell, William, 161
Preble, Ed, 63, 79
Protege, The, 166

Radio Stars magazine, 63, 87, 93
"Rah-Rah Boys", 20, 23
Rains, Claude, 169
Randall, Tony, 161
Raye, Martha, 148
Red Buttons Show, The, 149
Reiner, Carl, 159
Reisner, Charles, 88
Remy, Dick & Dotty, 120, 122
Requiem for a Heavyweight, 154-158, 175, 178
Reynolds, Debbie, 185
Ritz Brothers, 148
Rogers, Elmer, 20
Rogers, Ginger, 62
Rogers, Henry, 131
Rogers, Richard, 61
Rogers, Will, 46, 52
Romero, Caesar, 130
Rubber Heels, 54-55
Ruby, Harry, 88
Russon, Edmund, 29

Sahl, Mort, 165
Sales, Soupy, 7
Sands, Tommy, 178
San Francisco *Call*, 24
Schildkraut, Joseph, 171
Schubert Gaities of 1919, 40
Schumach, Murray, 177
Scooda Hay, 122
Sennett, Mack, 27, 167
Serling, Rod, 154-156, 175, 178
77 Sunset Strip, 179
Seven Year Itch, The, 161
Shaw, Hollis, 122

Shore, Dinah, 130, 169
Simon, Neil, 9
Simple Simon, 59-63
Six of a Kind, 91
Skelton, Red, 49, 145-146, 151, 153, 157,
178, 183, 185
Small, Paul, 112, 127
Smith & Dale, 110
Some Like It Hot, 161
Sometime, 39
Son of Flubber, 179
Sound of Laughter, The, 179
Stage Door Canteen, 112
Starr, Kay, 130
Stevens, George, 169, 171
Sullivan, Ed, 111, 127-128, 141, 151, 153
Swansen, Gloria, 130
Syracuse Journal, 23
Szomory, Dezo, 95
Szonys, The, 129

Texaco Command Performance, 168
Texaco Star Theater, 125-126, 134
Time magazine, 67, 111
Thurber-Nasher 10-20-30 Rep. Company, 12
The Chief, 88-90
This Is Your Life, 150
Thomas, Danny, 137
Thompson, Kay, 102
Three Stooges, The, 90, 130, 135, 161
To Be Or Not To Be, 91, 167
Todd, Thelma, 54, 90
Toledo *Blade*, 45
Tonight Show, The, 179
Torme, Mel, 130
Town Hall Tonight, 97
Tucker, Sophie, 110

TV Guide, 149
20th Century Fox Hour, The, 166
Twilight Zone, The, 175-176, 179-180

Vance, Vivian, 102-104
Van Dyke, Dick, 180, 185
Vanity Fair, 43
Variety magazine, 23, 30, 79, 140, 141, 182
154, 174
Vos, George W., 76

WEAF, 48
WJZ, 48
Weber & Fields, 52
Weber, Joe, 13
Welch, Joe, 13
Wences, Senior, 110
West, Mae, 39-40
When Comedy Was King, 162
White, George, 55-56
Williams, Bert, 32-33
Williams, William B., 185
Wilson, Don, 144
Winchell, Paul, 148
Winchell, Walter, 110
Winters, Jonathan, 165
Winters, Shelly, 171
Wizard of Oz, The, 98, 106
Wynn, Keenan, 12, 36-37, 52, 55-57, 69-70,
120, 127, 147, 150, 153, 155-158, 159, 177,
178, 183

You Bet Your Life (radio), 86, (TV), 149
Your Show of Shows, 149
Young, Loretta, 110
Young, Rita Johnson, 39
Youngman, Henny, 16

Ziegfeld, Florenz (Flo), 32, 44, 59, 62   Ziegfeld *Follies*, 4, 32-34

www.ingramcontent.com/pod-product-compliance
Lightning Source LLC
Chambersburg PA
CBHW071439150426
43191CB00008B/1185